Peacemaking and Dialogue

Peacemaking and Dialogue

Religious Approaches in the Quest for an Interfaith Relations

Edited by
Mar Pongener

Foreword by
A. Temjen Jamir

Clark Centre for Peace Research and Action (CCPRA)
Clark Theological College

&

Christian World Imprints™

CCPRA Publication Series No. 10

First Published in 2018 by

Clark Centre for Peace Research and Action (CCPRA)
Clark Theological College
Aolijen, Mokokchung 798601 / Nagaland
ctcprin@gmail.com
www.ctcnagaland.com
Phone: 09436006979

&

Christian World Imprints™
Christian Publishing & Books from India
H-12 Bali Nagar, New Delhi-110015
info@christianworldimprints.com
www.ChristianWorldImprints.com
Phone: +91 11 25465925

ISBN: 978-93-5148-311-3 (HB)
ISBN: 978-93-5148-312-0 (PB)

Printed in India.

Contents

Foreword

Engaging in dialogue towards peacemaking has been seen as life-changing and life-affirming efforts in the history of the human community. It requires openness, acceptance, understanding and respect for the other person, so that it may provide a fruitful result. In fact, in dialogue two people or two groups of people can come together in a face to face context to pour out and express their emotions and feelings spontaneously that aims at achieving a mutual understanding and long lasting solution to the existing problem. Today, as we live in a religiously pluralistic context in which different faith communities closely live together with one another, prejudices, intolerance, hatred and conflict can be occurred due to ideological and doctrinal differences, faith and truth claims among the different religious groups. It disturbs the peaceful atmosphere and strains relationships with one another. In this connection, dialogue has been found as one of the effective methods of promoting tolerance, reconciliation, interfaith-relation and peace among the people in the society. The seminar organised by the Clark Centre for Peace Research and Action (CCPRA) on November 18-19, 2016, aptly focused on the theme: *Peacemaking and Dialogue: Religious Approaches in the Quest for an Interfaith Relation,* from different perspectives such as biblical, theological, religious, historical, ethical, tribal and missiological perspectives. This effort will enlighten us with a wide range of knowledge and better understanding on how dialogue can be effectively used to deal with different human problems, in order to explore and promote peace and interfaith relation among different faith communities in the society.

Since its inception, the Clark Centre for Peace Research and Action has conducted a number of seminars on conflict and peacemaking in order to promote peace awareness-education and action among the people in the region and beyond. These seminar papers were edited and published under different titles in order to encourage wider readership and action on this area of concern; *Conflict and Peacemaking*. This volume focuses on Peacemaking and Dialogue, giving us new insights and perspectives on how the different religious approaches can be considered appropriately in the light of building peace initiatives and interfaith relation in the society. I would like to thank Rev. Dr. Mar Pongener for taking the responsibility and editing this volume in a proper manner. I hope that this volume will go to the lives of many people, especially the academic community and touch their hearts with commitment towards our common concern that is Conflict and Peacemaking. May this book be a source of blessing for many people so also to be channels of peace to others in their own respective place.

Rev. Dr. A. Temjen Jamir
Academic Dean
Clark Theological College

Acknowledgements

The present volume is the outcome of a two-day national seminar organized by Clark Centre for Peace Research and Action (CCPRA), Clark Theological College on 18th and 19th November, 2016. Papers that were presented during the seminar were Biblical perspectives, Ethics of Interfaith Cooperation, Religious Sociology and Interfaith relations, Tribal religious perspective on Interfaith, Missiological perspective on Dialogue, and concept of the 'other' from the Hindu and Christian perspective. The seminar was attended by representatives from different religious traditions in and across the region. The thought provoking papers presented by various scholars have made the members to know more about the importance of peacemaking and to be more aware of the issues involved in the process of peacemaking. Thus, the CCPRA committee decided to compile those scholarly papers into a book.

My sincere gratitude goes to Ms. C. Pursenla Ozukum, former program coordinator of the CCPRA, under whose initiatives the seminar was conducted. Her sincerity and wholehearted service rendered towards CTC and particularly to the CCPRA is appreciated. I wish her success as she pursue her Doctoral Study. Thanks go to the members of the CCPRA committee for giving me the honor to edit this book. I truly appreciate Ms. Imtiwala Imchen, Program Coordinator CCPRA, for her sincere assistance. I express sincere thanks to all the contributors of the articles for their scholarly works and researches. Finally, sincere appreciation to the EMW, Germany for their generous support through which all the peace related activities undertaken by the CCPRA since inception would have not been possible.

I am also grateful to the Christian World Imprints, New Delhi, for publishing our books.

May God bless everyone who has made the publication of this book a success.

Blessings!

Mar Pongener
Editor

Introduction

Mar Pongener

Talks about peace and the need for peace has always been a widespread topic. Peace is a stage of nurturing harmony, order and concord. Why peace? Individually, to grow to our full measure and socially, to bring up our families, to develop our nations and to work towards the total well-being of all. Peace is a gift from God, a gift to be yearned for, enjoyed, shared and practiced. Peacemaking grows from the humble suspicion that our own perspective is limited and that there are truths we can discover if we listen. It requires flexibility of our thoughts and to have the willingness to see different views to an issue more openly by engaging in dialogue with different people.

In this book, the CCPRA has published the works of scholars and writers who in their understanding has written chapters on Peacemaking and Dialogue, focused more towards the aspect of interfaith relations.

Everyone individually, needs to create an environment that prides itself on the commitment to peace, unity and interfaith dialogue. We sincerely have to believe that it can be fixed. We have to also submit to the fact that we have to cultivate a society of acceptance with our neighbours regardless of religion. As a society, we need to begin to initiate conversations and relations with one another to strive and grow as faith communities.

The chapters that comprise this book brings to readers enough points and illustrations on the need to develop interfaith religion and dialogue. Varied from different biblical points and cultural aspects, readers will be able to relate and hopefully realise the need of giving peace a chance and also understand the beauty of establishing interfaith relations with ones neighbours.

Dealing with religious approaches for Interfaith Relations, Packiam T. Samuel in his keynote address brings out the beauty of our world today, a world of diversity and immensity, a world our God created. He writes about how people are affected by human advancements and more importantly, by religion based beliefs. He brings to light the plan of God for the World and talks about 'How?' and 'Why?' people should establish varied human communities among themselves, or as he writes, the 'other'. The chapter further brings thoughts and questions on whether God's mission for the transformation of the world is possible or rather inevitable. The writer discusses and brings out how one must be able to adopt various beliefs and attitudes and also to rebuild one's paradigm of life to fulfil God's mission. He proposes and enlightens readers with a number of steps and methods; transformative means, that one can adopt to bring forth the fulfilment of God's vision. He writes paragraphs about how Christians should understand the variants of faith and religion emphasizing on the misconception Christians have of the two. The chapter ends with notes on characteristics of God; who He is, what He is, His nature and His varied laudable traits, inspiring and challenging readers to imitate Jesus and become agents of transformation for the new world, a God-filled world.

The first chapter by S. Dhane Zhemai, a biblical scholar, makes an attempt to bring a functional understanding of God by studying some of the divine designations in the Old Testament. She does an in-depth study of '*Yahweh*' and '*Elohim*', which were one of many names God was known as, in the Old Testament. She does this to illustrate the nature, personality and character of God. With references from passages in the Old Testament, she attempts to develop a 'Christian Understanding of God'; to better learn about God and his ways through his own self-revelation. She chooses to use the word '*Hesed*' to further define and understand God's love; by referring to passages in the Old Testament and also from books by other authors.

The second chapter by Woba James, with his paper entitled 'Peacemaking and Dialogue in the History of Christianity', primarily looks into the history of peacemaking and dialogue initiatives by the church to the society. He talks about peacemaking and dialogue and their various content and approaches on instances from our world today. He also surveys its relation with the history of the church; till 600 A.D, till the Reformation and during the post-reformation. He continues to write about the proceeds of peacemaking and dialogue between the Western and Eastern Christianity till the 19th century and also the efforts put in by the church till this day. He brings to light valid histories and stories related to peacemaking and dialogue all throughout the above mentioned years and time. He then brings a focus on present India; talking about religious turmoil, importance of dialogues in a multi religious society and so forth. He also presents a detailed list of concluded meetings and seminars between churches, associations, groups, etc.; all of whom carried out the process of inter-faith dialogue in India and decided to work on that common importance. Furthermore, he highlights on the essentiality of inter-faith dialogue in a country like India; a country divided by communal conflict. Ending the chapter reflecting on the Bible and relating it with God and Christians, the writer offers valid statements and examples for us to understand a Christian's role in peacemaking and dialogue.

The third chapter by S. Hayong, links interfaith relations to a pluralistic society; a society with people from different races, communities and people with different political or religious beliefs. He sheds light on the pluralistic nature of the Indian society and goes on to write about how 'Pluralism' can be viewed as a positive feature in society and not something that would hinder peaceful co-existence in a diverse society. The writer also writes about 'Religious Pluralism', where people of different faiths co-exist together in their attempt to find the ultimate truth. All in all, he presents an array of different topics, from politics to theologies on interfaith relations, bringing out the importance of peaceful and harmonious living in a pluralistic society that would eventually lead to transformation and to the growth of a nation.

The fourth chapter by Eyingbeni Hümtsoe-Nienu, focuses on the primal/indigenous tribal religions of Northeast India. She tries to bring out trans-religious values and also suggestions to achieve and reformulate a perspective for inter-religious harmony, focusing on the primal tribal worldview. She writes about traditional beliefs and conceptual thinkings, giving readers an idea of the lives of the tribal people. The writer relates to the primal worldview to challenge religious attitudes that hinder human relations; she does this by writing about ideals and nature of the primal tribal people. All in all, the writer brings out how the essence of tribal worldview can actually transform relationships and make co-existence less fanatic; be it with God, or even with other people.

Rather similar to the earlier chapter by S. Hayong, Rongsen Longkumer in the fifth chapter talks about a religiously plural world with focus on the challenges and problems of living in such a society. He also reflects on an ethical point of view in relation to theology using references from different scholars to conclude that religious pluralism has to be affirmed, celebrated, cherished and nurtured. The sixth chapter by Prabhakar Bhattacharyya attempts to bring out the concept of 'the other' in the mind-set of the contemporary Hindus. He gives basic introductions to the understanding of human 'mind-set' and also highlights on the history and present scenario of Hinduism in India. The entire chapter is written with focus on Hinduism in India; its religion, beliefs, tradition, rituals and practices all of which concludes to the importance to understand and work together through religious pluralism. In the seventh chapter C. Pursenla Ozukum, writes about Maulana Wahiduddin Khan's approach and understanding to building a peaceful community and his principle of following one religion and respecting all others. She also includes his beliefs and teachings in relation to Islam and the Quran, all implying to fighting the differences that hinder peaceful living with different communities and Khan's vision of co-existence and ultimately achieving peace.

The eight chapter by Dhanbir Rai, talks about the practice of '*Guthi*' by the 'newars'. A practice he learnt about from his trip to Nepal, a practice that maintains healthy interfaith and moral order among the 'newars'. He talks about the beliefs, traditions and moral ideologies of 'newars' and their quest of maintaining peace among themselves irrespective of religion and caste. With much emphasis on *Guthi* institutions, he illustrates about the teachings of *Guthi* that bind the newars together at the three different levels of caste, patrilineal grouping and territory. He concludes with lines on how *Guthis* promote a sense ideology that regulates religious and moral order in public as well as in the spiritual realm and how they have been instrumental in removing religious and social divisions, to rather promote social solidarity.

The ninth chapter by Jayakumar Ramachandran, is an attempt by the writer with a Christian outlook, to reconcile the social need for sustainable peace among the multi-religious people of India and to retain the exclusive epistemological significances of religions. The nine presuppositions are the premise for the enhancement of this paper. He first makes readers understand that 'Peacemaking' is the core purpose of the mission of the God of the Bible. He further analyses the role of interfaith dialogue in the peacemaking process in the past followed by the role of the Church. His analysis leads him to insist on a need for broad and sustainable peacemaking and peace-prevailing mechanisms in India. The conclusion is further supported by presenting five setbacks in the dialogue strategy and brings six suggestions to the religious groups for their way forward. His elucidation comes to an end by challenging the non-Christian and Christian religions to respond to his call for peacemaking and peace prevalence among the religious groups without diluting their respective epistemological values and significances. Yakubu Tanko Jakada, in the tenth chapter lays main emphasis on 'The truth and Reconciliation Commission' in South Africa, a project focused and aimed at bring healing and reconciliation those oppressed under the regime of apartheid in South Africa and reconciliation in the state of Kaduna in Nigeria, a state plagued by violence and religious division amidst distrust and anger. He also analyses the state of Apartheid in South Africa; its establishment, major laws that were passed that formed what became apartheid and experiences of the native South Africans. He further details the history, characteristics and progress of the TRC and also sheds light on the ethno-religious violence in the state of Kaduna. In conclusion, the writer draws a few points on the success and impact of the TRC in promoting reconciliation and national unity.

The final chapter by Toshi Aier brings to readers some of the basic features that build Interfaith Dialogue. He initially writes about the essentiality of Interfaith Dialogue to make readers discover, promote and celebrate the reality of pluralism and to promote greater understanding between people of different religions. He brings to the readers, the forms and characteristics of dialogue, explaining the importance and variability of each. He further writes about various different factors that challenge Interfaith Dialogue particularly in India. He also mentions the history and the programs of the World Council of Churches (WCC) in its aim of establishing interfaith dialogue. He concludes with a set of recommendations for conduct on Christian witness around the world with relation to the document, 'Christian Witness in a Multi-Religious world'.

Keynote Address

Packiam T. Samuel[1]

God Created a Beautiful World

It is beautiful for many reasons. To mention a few; the great diversity in creation; every item, whether a flower, a plant or an animal, a bird or a human being is uniquely fashioned and God creates no duplicates. Beautiful because in spite of such great diversity and immensity, they all are inter-connected and inter-dependent. The connection being organic and internal, not mechanical, through bolts and nuts. Beautiful because there is so much harmony and sharing, both giving and receiving and all of it without charge. Beautiful because the God-created world is an abundant world, there is no scarcity.

Our World Today

We live today in a wonder world, a world of super human performances that we have made happen. Steven Kotler, in his book, *Superhuman Performances* says that in the last few decades (not centuries) more new appliances, products and processes have been invented and made available than in the past 150,000 years of human history. There is however a shadow side to this, that this abundance of gadgets and conveniences is available only to a few. The majority of people experience various kinds of severe scarcities and pain, arising from poverty, ill health, joblessness, and ugly forms of violence and terror acts. Imagine a visit of Martians, who are experts from several disciplines, who, having heard of

1 Rev. Dr. Packiam T. Samuel, is the Director, Henry Martyn Institute, Hyderabad, India.

the great human achievements, want to verify and come on a visit. They are happily surprised to find that all they heard is true and more than true. However, when some of them take out time to talk to individuals, to family members, to those in institutions such as schools, hospitals and those in business, they find that many are experiencing severe forms of pain. One major source for the pain, violence and suffering, including numerous deaths, comes from religion-based belief systems. Some others are ideologies, ethnic and regional differences, and most of all, the growing inequality created by globalization. Abundance is for a few and even they are not happy. But the majority experience scarcity. That is why the search for a just and egalitarian world order as an alternative to the present paradigm has become an urgent imperative.

God's Plan and God's Mission for the World

Does God want us to live in this state of misery? Live in a valley of tears till we get to heaven? Definitely no. If you see heaven as a state and not as a place, can we begin to create in some small but real measure, the experience of wellness and joy or heaven on earth, using all the great endowments that we have been blessed with? The single mission that Jesus undertook was to create what He called the establishment of the Reign of God on earth. Namely that God's will should prevail on earth as it does in heaven. He initiated it through a small group of disciples and inspired them with vision and mission to carry forward the mission. Countless others have since picked up what they had done and continued the mission of God of building a new world. I propose that engaging in Dialogue is an effective way to bring wellness and joy of life, not just for a few, but for many, for most and indeed for all.

Building a Cross-Border Human Community is a Christian Imperative

I can conclude that I cannot be a Christian, a follower of Christ, if I do not want to have any contact with the "other" and want to live and relate only to those in my small circle of life. Our engaging with the "other" is a spiritual imperative of our Christian faith. Of the several things that are unique in our Christian faith, one of them is the emphasis on linking with the "other" or what the gospel calls linking with our neighbor. To the question; who is my neighbor? The gospel answer; my neighbors are not only those at home or my friends and relatives, those of my own religion, culture or region but also "others". The parable of the Good Samaritan is a foundational parable of the gospel spirituality of building human communities across borders that divide us. In Mt 25, there is a telling narrative of who gets a ticket and becomes eligible to enter the Kingdom of God. Only those who found it possible to reach out to the 'other' are eligible. Therefore, Christian mission can be understood as building human communities across those borders that presently divide us and which make us less and less human.

Is this Transformation of Our World Possible?

The answer is an emphatic Yes. Jesus presented a great vision and mission for the transformation of the world. To the young and the older people, a great vision and mission creates great passion. But to achieve this great mission, we need to go beyond a few talks and seminars and adopt dialogue as our paradigm, as *our way of life.* How can this be done? Change our present attitudes. 'The greatest discovery of our generation', said William James, 'is that we can change our lives by changing our attitudes'. Alvin Toffler said that "the illiterates of the 21st century are not those who cannot read and write but those who are unwilling to *Learn*, to *Unlearn* and to *Relearn.*"How do we adopt dialogue as our new way of life? By changing our present attitudes, habits and behavioral patterns. How can we do this? By our willingness to *Learn,* to *Unlearn* and to *Relearn*. These three are critical words that can bring a startling transformation. This is greatly being manifested in our present history in the field of science and technology. The great invitation from God; introduce a new paradigm also in the other sectors of life as well, through dialogue.

Our Belief Systems and Our Paradigms Define Our Lives

Attitude is my inner lens, through which I habitually see reality and my habitual way of responding to reality (that reality may be persons, things, conditions, etc.). We can say that attitude is everything. These beliefs and attitudes evolve into a paradigm for our life and living. All of us have a paradigm for our life and living. Why does our belief system or paradigm define our lives? It enables us to do something easily what someone else may find very hard to do. Is it important that we follow a paradigm? Yes, because a paradigm defines the goals and purposes of our lives. It clarifies to us the "whys of my life" or the reasons "why we are doing""what we are doing or not doing." It explains why we make a decision or take a new direction in life. It provides us with a 'road map' for our life, to enable us to navigate through the ever-changing roads and pathways of life. It gives us a frame of reference; a lens through which to view life and which provides us a model that guides our decisions and patterns of behavior. It also becomes the source of energy and motive power for our life and actions. Therefore, our success and happiness comes from the kind of beliefs we have.

Revise Our Maps

Our view of reality (our paradigm) is like a map with which to negotiate the terrains of life. We are not born with maps, we have to make them and the making requires effort. Our maps, made earlier, go out of date and we need to revise maps. Making revisions, especially major revisions, is very painful, sometimes excruciatingly painful. And herein lies the major source of many of the ills of humankind. How to bring about a change in my life? Is that what defines and directs my life, my belief system? Who am I and why am I here on earth are questions for which we must have a clear personal answer. From early childhood, we receive many directions, advices, warnings, etc., many do's and don'ts coming from significant people; our parents and other important family members, from priests or gurus to teachers and others, which we internalize and which forms our belief system. These also contribute to form several of our stereotypes. A stereotype is a shorthand in our patterns of thought and images and which often are translated into social behavior and responses.

Having created a wonder world with our many technological inventions, many or most still thirst for something more, something deeper and something spiritual. We need Information and Communications Technology (ICT) in our life but we need more than just ICT devices if we have to experience wellness and the joys of life. In spite of all the advances, life often confronts us with its mediocrity, its sameness and mere repeats of our yesterdays. How to renew and re-energize our whole life and re-kindle a fire in our hearts? How to discover and execute a new way of being me? A new way to make a difference in life through my positive actions and contributions? How to become an active partner to build a new world? How to contribute to bring about a spiritual awakening? Living in a dialogical way is a new and self-transforming way to live that new life. When you actually discover and practice some of the new and specific ways and responses to life each day, you will surely experience magic.

Four Point Mantra Solution: Make Dialogue a Transformative Way of Life

We will explore some active steps to make dialogue a transformative way of life and living. By making dialogue a paradigm for our life and living, as a new way of being Me, being Us, I suggest a four word mantra solution to bring about this transformation of life and living. These four action words are: ***Believe, Connect, Stretch and Eliminate.*** We humans are multi-dimensional and so, the formula is also multi-dimensional and holistic. This four-word solution can be made applicable to all spheres of our life: personal life, family life, business life, institutional life or spiritual life.

Believe: Believe in God. Who is the God that I believe in? It would seem fair to say that God is probably the most misunderstood and misrepresented person. We make so many cartoons of God. God created a beautiful world and He wants to restore the integrity of His creation by inviting us to partner in that restoration process through dialogue. Few quotes from the Bible's account of creation are noteworthy to mention. Genesis 1 and 2 portrays creation as it came from the creator's hand, namely in a perfect state. All human needs were provided for and man, woman and God lived together in perfect harmony. They trusted each other and enjoyed each other's company, walking together in the Garden of Eden in the cool of the day. This golden state was abruptly brought to an end by human disobedience when Adam and Eve ate the forbidden fruit. This disobedience and rebellion led to their expulsion from the garden.

The Lord God is the source and origin of everything and of everyone, the God of abundance, compassion and love. This is the beautiful narrative of creation in the Bible, written in the literary format of a story. We are spiritual beings. We are a soul with also a body. God and the rest of creation are in perfect harmony. This is the harmony we humans are invited to contribute and create in order to become partners in the mission of God. In the God world, everything is connected, organically and intrinsically. Recreating that paradigm is the goal and mission of dialogue, given to us humans. A great privilege and challenge!

It demands that we make new beliefs, new paradigms, and new maps. Believe that God has a great mission for us and we will feel fulfilled only when we willingly and enthusiastically partner in that mission. Believe in the diversity of nature and humans as part of God's own design and purpose and accept and appreciate differences; Believe that all, yes everyone, whom God has created, are precious to Him and He saves all His people.

Believe in Myself: Uniquely designed and fashioned by God, who believes in you and makes no duplicates. Believe that God created you and everyone else out of love. When this belief is deep and does not remain merely as a notion at the top of my mind but it rather gets anchored in my heart and spirit, it transforms me. Then miracles of all sizes will begin to happen; small, medium and large. The Ayurveda insight; "what the mind sees, the body does." There is a great deal of research being done on the brain and many programs have been developed to enable miracles to happen through this self-love, self-appreciation and self-belief. "Who am I?" is a question that Indian seekers and saints have sought for an answer for thousands of years. The answer is still controlled largely by amygdala in our brain, issuing many inhibitions and cautions. I can break free and can become courageous to produce deeds of light. How positive am I about myself? Do I say that I am not good enough or that I am good enough? It is a great source of strength that God, who created everyone, believes in each and has made us partners in His mission. Break the myth that genius is the prerogative of a few, of very few. You are uniquely fashioned. There is a one-on-one involvement of God withyou. You have a contribution to make to life, to make a difference and leave a legacy. To attain this great objective, we need plenty of additional support. That is the next area of belief. You are not alone and you have a great deal of additional support available.

Believe in Others: Each of them also uniquely fashioned, which creates the awesome diversity and beauty of life. Believe that many are ready to accompany you on your journey through life, though some may not agree. Discover those people rather than focus on the ones who do not extend a helping hand. Create synergy, by linking your energy with those of others and creating a new energy that is much bigger than what you with all your ability and hard work can produce. Produce the miracle of 1+1= not 2 but 3 or 4 or more.

Believe in the Contexts and Conditions of Life: Life that offers you many opportunities to produce these miracles. Recognize that all the constituents of the universe are inter-connected and that you can plug into this boundless resource and produce deeds of light. Thus, Paulo Coelho's insight: "when you desire something with all your heart, the whole world would move to help you attain it."

Connect: Connect is a key word, a focus word, a foundational action word for internalizing the dialogue paradigm or map. Whether I am a connecting or a disconnecting person determines the quality of my wellness, my winning in life or my losing and my being accepted or avoided. Our present world is fully connected globally through internet, mobile phones, TVs, radios and many more. In spite of the mechanical and electronic connection, there is a growing lack of emotional bonding and the distance between us is growing. God is the most connecting and connected person, connected with everyone and everything. Happy and successful persons are those who have established good interpersonal connections. More than money, we earnestly desire to connect emotionally, to have warm and affectionate relationships. That is our quest.

Stretch: Life is difficult as it brings us many problems. But it is when we face and solve these problems that we grow mentally and spiritually. This demands discipline. To deal constructively with problems and the suffering it carries, we need discipline. The true measure of your greatness is revealed not from how you behave in times of comfort and security but how you respond when you face a googly from life. Most persons choose to remain in the comfort zone of a small personal circle that they have created and ignore the call to break out to the frontiers beyond. This is due to our unwillingness to stretch, the reluctance to face the pain of stretching and so live a life that is small. Growth and progress in any domain are not possible without the discipline of stretching, excelling and of going beyond traditional borders and boundaries. To make dialogue as a way of life, we need to stretch.

Eliminate: How ready are we to accept that our wellness or illness is largely an *inside job,* that it is we who largely create our illness in our body? We carry many kinds of baggage inside us, feelings and attitudes that can result in many forms of illness. Eliminate anything and everything that should not be stored inside you. If you don't, it will rot inside and cause you 'indigestion' and will make you ill. "The mother of all diseases is indigestion" is an Ayurvedic insight. So, eliminate fear which causes so many 'deaths' before one finally dies. Eliminate Anger which poisons your body and soul. Eliminate resentments which can dissolve even cancer. Eliminate the habit of living in the past (which is no more real now) or in the future (which is yet to be). Instead, live in the Now of your life. How ready are we to accept that our wellness or illness is largely an inside job, that it is we who largely create our illness in our body? We carry many kinds of baggage inside us, feelings and attitudes that can result in many forms of illness.

Assuming Dialogue as a Paradigm is a Spiritual Choice

What makes the dialogue way of life spiritual? It is spiritual when we are responding to the plan of God to re-create a new world, a world where God's will and purpose will be done on earth as it is in heaven. It is spiritual when we become strengthened by the grace of God to stretch beyond traditional relationships and stereotypes and are able to cross narrow borders to connect with all members of the human family as members of the great family of God. It is spiritual when we find the courage to eliminate long-held and disease-causing feelings and sentiments such as resentment, anger, fear, etc., and are ready to forgive others and self. It is spiritual when we form new attitudes and habits that make us deeply human and hence also truly share in God's divinity.

THE GOD MYSTERY – Faith vs Religion Perspectives

We live in a world where many people avoid reference to God or a higher power. These people are God shy, we might say. But the majority of people have some form or another of a belief system in their life. There is a felt need in the heart of many, who are searching for that something more that will fulfil their lives, in spite of the tremendous progress we have made and the affluence of life they enjoy. Spiritual is in. Meditation is sought after. God, declared dead earlier, is beginning to get resurrected again. It is in that context that I will join in that search for God. As we will have presentations from different faith traditions, I will present from the Christian tradition.

Christian theology says that the authors and editors of the Bible were led or influenced or inspired by God with the result that their writings can be designated in some sense as the word of God. There is a special revelation contained in these books. Biblical scholars see a dual authorship in every book: one the human author, divinely inspired, but with all his natural talents, background and mindsets and the divine author, God. Every book has been thoroughly researched, subjecting it to historical text criticism or hermeneutics. The Bible remains the most researched text in the world. Truth can stand scrutiny, even minute scrutiny.

The Gift of Jesus to us - A New Religion or a New Spirituality?

The question is often asked, "*Did Jesus come to start a new religion or to teach us to live a new faith?*"We search for an answer. *Who is God and what is He like* are fundamental questions whose answer every religion seeks. All religions have two parts: an inner part and an outer part, a faith part or God part and a religion part. What constitutes the substance and essence of a religion is the inner core, its faith constituent, its vision, its spirituality and fundamental God-view which provide direction for life and living. These inner parts consist of God-inspired and Spirit-directed insights regarding who God is and of His relationship with all others and with the world around. Ritualized prayer recitations, ceremonies, festivals and prescriptions and rules, etc., form the outer part, as well as clarification and definition of articles of faith. The answer to the fundamental question, who is God? can be a religion-based one from our human vision and experiences or from a faith inspired revelation from God, as expressed in the scripture. Religions differ in both aspects, in the faith-based beliefs and in religious practices. I will mention a unique revelation about the faith gift that Jesus brought us, His Good News to us: the unconditional and gratuitous love of God for everyone who came from His loving heart. This is the foundational revelation of our faith. Everything else is footnotes. The Gospel that Jesus brought is an attitude revolution, a vision revolution and a relationship revolution. If we turn it into a mere religion and rituals, we have lost the gift of Jesus.

We are called to faith, not to religion. If Christians do not understand this, they fail to understand the very heart of the Christian message. Christianity is a call to faith. Faith is the joining of man or woman with God in intimate communion. On the other hand, religion is a human construct. And yet, religion remains the most attractive coping mechanism for the majority of people today. This phenomenon is not new. Fear-driven religion has always coexisted with the call to intimacy with God, which is faith. Religion is much older than faith, in fact as old as the humans. We create religion for the same reason that we fashion anything else, to meet a human need. We produce religions and religion substitutes to enable us better to cope with the uncertainties of life and to deal with its dangers. Fear has played a major part in the origin and evolution of different religions. This fear dimension is fully exploited for profit. The revelation of Jesus invites us to break free of this fear. We hear this in the Old Testament of the Bible. Repeatedly we hear this repeated by Jesus in the Gospel: '*Don't be afraid. I am with you*'. When Yahweh God of the Hebrews called Abraham to a faith life, religion pre-existed. Faith was the novelty. Unless we become fully aware, we will be relating to God religiously, not through faith. We have a natural tendency not to let go of elements of religion, even when we are striving to be people of faith. Israel was warned again and again not to get the religiosity and religions of the peoples around to taint their faith. Neither the warning of Yahweh nor of the prophets could prevent the Israelites from the mixing of elements from other religions, so that what we see in the Old Testament is a strange amalgam of faith and religion, resulting often in a strange caricature of God. We are facing the same now among Christians, since much of what passes for renewal is, on closer inspection, a reassertion of religiosity, not of faith. By faith we put aside our fears and our self-interest and commit ourselves to become a partner with God to build the new world, or what Jesus called the Kingdom of God on earth.

Here is a good process definition of the Kingdom: "building human communities across all those borders that presently divide us and which make us less and less human and hence less and less divine."We do need borders and identities. But push those too much and we become less and less human and we will soon resemble the animals we witness in the Animal Planet. Both old and present events of our history amply illustrate the degree of human degradation that is taken place.

Do we then need religion? Yes, as a support system, not as a takeover mechanism. Do we need this support, these many devotional practices? Yes. Jesus wonders aloud whether the Son of Man will find any faith on earth when he returns (Lk 18:8).

Religion is a structured human response to transcendence. The Gospel provides a new lens, a new paradigm, a new way of seeing and relating to God, to self and to others, a radical shift from religion to faith. But often, we prefer to stay with the old and the familiar.

The human Jesus, as a perceptive bright young man, began to gain insight into where the religion of his fathers had descended to. So much of mere frozen ritualism had crept in; such multiplication of rules and rituals introduced as necessary to become holy; so much of commercialization of the sacred had taken place!! He could see how the Scribes, the Pharisees and the lawyers were making it impossible for people to be in touch with God and to become spiritual because of the over-emphasis on the outer. The result? Religion, meant to reveal God, had masked the face of God! The exact observance of the letter of the law was prescribed as the only way leading to salvation. But his own experience, through personal prayer, revealed to him God as a Father, as *Abba*, who is close, who is tender, full of compassion and mercy. So, Jesus replaced *fear*, which has been the driving force in religion with *love*. This was the paradigm shift from religion to spirituality, from rituals to faith. From mere external or self-seeking and self-preserving motives that animated many practices of religion, He began to show the way to God through a new way of living, a new spirituality, the spirituality of relationships or communion. Hence, the startling new focus by Jesus; in and through community alone lies our salvation! You can't skip others and get to God.

Some Indicators whether Religion Predominates in Our Life

How do we discern the degree of religion that has entered our life and how religion is creating a casualty of the faith gift from Jesus? Professor Dick Westley, in his book, *Redemptive Intimacy*, describes seven characteristics to assess the degree of religion in our life. One or two may co-exist in a person of faith but if they all co-exist, then faith has become a casualty. The seven characteristics are; 1. Do I relate to God out of *fear*? 2. Do I feel the need to appease an *angry* God? 3. Do I relate to God out of *self-interest*, to get benefits and favors from God and even attempt to get Him to do my will? 4. Do I view myself as *unworthy* in God's sight? We are obviously unworthy, but the Gospel (good news) is that we are loved and cherished by God as His precious sons and daughters and so, are made worthy by God. 5. Do I hold that there are *two worlds,* one in which we live and another, far away, in which God dwells? 6. Do I hold that some things in the world, e.g. sex, pleasure, fun, celebrations, etc., are evil or at least that God is not very happy or comfortable with them? Or do we believe that *all that came through His loving heart are good, in fact, very good?* 7. Do I violate the freedom and personhood of another by doing physical or psychological harm and justify doing so '*in the name of God'?*

Each of these items contradicts an element essential to being a person of faith. We are surprised to see how much of religion still exists in us and also the amount of religiosity in our Christian practices. When not diluted by religion, faith remains the most powerful force on earth for transformation, for love and for giving us freedom of choice and action. This is the heartbeat of our faith. If this heart beat stops, faith dies.

A fear-filled people can never truly be God's people, for they can never be truly the sign people, which is an essential characteristic of our Christian vocation. As religion gets institutionalized over time, the gap grows between religion and spirituality. Religion tends to get ritualized, mechanized, routinized and so, religion becomes an obstacle to spirituality. Religion, which is meant to help open the face of God to us, often *becomes a veil that masks the face of God. Religion becomes a defense mechanism.* The inner dynamism and the heart of religion, its meaning and mission, get dissipated in a whole lot of activities, most of them economic and secular. In this process, faith becomes the casualty, as religion alienates us from our true self, from others, from genuine relationships and from God himself, the root and anchor of our life.

Today, with young people, this religious version of Christianity carries little credit and so many are leaving the Church. Three reasons were given; they get no God experience, they do not see proper reverence given to the Word of God and there is no focus on fellowship or community, a Christian imperative. A loving and forgiving community, which is a grace we receive from Faith, is replaced by competition and acts of domination and violence and an over-riding desire to *have control*, to exercise power and retain privileges. We then become no different from those whom we call politicians, business people, etc., or other categories of people. We have today too much of body and not enough of spirit; too much of religion and too little of spirituality; too much of the outer and too little of the inner. We need both, but the outer must be integrated with the inner. This is the call from Jesus today as during His historic life on earth; a conversion of heart and adoption of a new lifestyle, of the gospel paradigm.

The God of Faith

The other perspective is derived from Faith. We seek this in scripture, listening to God speaking to us through His word. Apophatic or negative theology affirms that we can describe God only in negative terms. We can, on the other hand, using analogy, describe God from what is revealed in the Bible with the understanding that the 'God mystery' is above and beyond what we can describe. *Deus simper major,* a mystery that we cannot comprehend, but believe in. St. Paul defines faith thus; "the guarantee of the things we hope for, and the certainty of the things that we do not see". Faith gives more than certainty. Dealing with God is different from every other relationship. So, we need to approach this encounter with profound humility, acknowledging our ignorance and our readiness to surrender to the mystery of God. Christians believe that there is only one God. But they also believe in the Trinity; God the Father, God the Son and God the Holy Spirit. Philosophy and theology are used to offer some explanations but we are dealing with a mystery. We have committed the sin of arrogance, claiming that we have the truth, the whole truth and nothing but the truth and others don't have it; a foolish attempt to make God our proprietary possession.

We get some insight into this God mystery through what Jesus reveals in the Gospel, through what he says, by the parables that He uses, the miracles that He works and by the modeling He does. His own lifestyle; his paradigm of life, his response to life conditions and to people provide us with some insights into the nature of the 'God mystery'. I will use some quotes from the Bible to find answers to the question; who is God and what is God like? God is love (1 Jn 4.7-21) God is compassionate and merciful (Gen 18.20-32). The gentle nature of God (1 Kgs 19.11-13). God's personal love for Me (Jn 15.9-10). God has no outsiders, all are precious to Him (Lk 14.12-14) Small is also beautiful for God (Lk 21:1-4). God has no untouchables; all are insiders (Lk 17:11-19). God who is ready to heal our ills (Lk 5:12-16). God has no enemies; God forgives; He is good to all (Luke 23:34). God is savior (Jn 3: 16-17).

Conclusion

I will close by quoting Pope John Paul II. He had conducted an inter-faith prayer meeting in Assisi in October. There was media criticism that the Pope has done something wrong, praying with non-Christians. He remained silent but in December, he referred to the criticism and said that he would only make this directional statement: "*What unites is divine; what divides is not*". Where there is unity, God is present. Where there is division, God is absent. It is this God mystery that Jesus presented to the people to imitate and He himself modeled His life. When we do this and imitate Jesus, we too become agents of transformation to create a new world, a God-filled world. That is the call. That is the challenge.

1

A Functional Understanding of God
Old Testament Perspective

S. Dhane Zhemai[1]

Introduction

We live in a multi-scriptural context where every religion talks about peace and reconciliation for peaceful co-existence in the society. People talk about peace, think about peace and work about peace, yet we still struggle to find peace. One of the reasons for stagnant transformation in bringing peace and harmony is failure in understanding the true concept of God and failing in carrying out His love in the society. In fact, understanding God in all His fullness is impossible, God is infinitely beyond our understanding (Job 36:26). However, that does not mean we should avoid the subject totally. God had made known to us through His traits and attributes.

Frequently, God in the Old Testament has been portrayed as a cruel and ruthless deity that indiscriminately orders the execution of seemingly innocent men, women, and children, or directly carries out their deaths by various means. Such a God, the argument goes, in no way represents the loving Creator or Father figure that the New Testament offers, and should in no way be worshipped

1 Ms. S. Dhane Zhemai is Lecturer of the Department of Old Testament, Witter Theological College, Wokha.

or venerated. However, a closer examination of Yahweh in the Old Testament refutes the charge of the Creator being a tyrant and instead reveals a righteous, patient, merciful, and loving God who does indeed mirror the picture painted by Jesus and the rest of the New Testament writers. Hence, in this paper an attempt is made to bring a functional understanding of God in the Old Testament by studying some of the divine designations and also how His love is portrayed to bring transformation and peaceful co-existence in the society.

1. Divine Designations in the Old Testament

Throughout the Scripture, God reveals to us through His names. When we study these names that He reveals to us in the Bible, we will better understand who God really is. The meanings behind God's names reveal the central personality and nature of the One who bears them. In the ancient world, names communicated something about a person's character, so a name carried much meaning with it. The meanings behind God's names reveal the central personality and nature of the One who bears them. God in the Old Testament has been known through many names yet the presenter will concentrate more on *Yahweh* and *Elohim*.

YAHWEH: *Yahweh* is the promised name of God. It is referred to as the Tetragrammaton.[2] Observant Jews do not pronounce the Tetragrammaton as the name is considered too sacred to be used, including in prayer and through reading sacred texts. There is nothing in the Torah to prohibit the saying of the name but even in ancient times, the name was only pronounced once a year by the high priest. Jews and those who wish to show respect will read the name as *Adonai* or *ha shem* (literally 'The Name'). A Jew will not even casually write the name God, not because it is prohibited but because in writing down the name, it may give rise to disrespectful pronunciation by another person. In respect of these views, this text always uses the form YHWH for the name of God.

2 The term Tetragrammaton is a Greek term that means "four-letter word" הוהי and refers to the traditional way of writing the name of God- YHWH.

While *YHWH* is first used in Gen. 2, God did not reveal Himself as *YHWH* until Ex. 3. YHWH is viewed usually as the 'proper name' for the God of Israel and is used over 6000 times[3] in the Hebrew Bible, including citations in verses where the term is used more than once or where it is used in combination with other divine titles such as Elohim. The term serves to distinguish God from the gods of other nations.[4] The original pronunciation is uncertain as this was lost from Jewish tradition sometime in the Middle Ages[5] but the pronunciation Yahweh has been recovered in modern times.

The exact meaning or, indeed, definition of the term is unclear. Most modern scholars would connect the term with the verb היה (*hayah*) which means to be, to become, to happen. Albright insists that YHWH is from the causative conjunction of this verb and means, 'he causes to be.'[6] Albright states how he and Freedman[7] highlighted that the name is a fragment of a longer name that translates as 'he who brings into being whatever comes into being'. The name explained thus identifies YHWH very clearly as the Creator. The name Yahweh is best known from

3 This is of course an approximation based on searching using the computer program "Bibleworks" as well as references to texts that concur with this number, including Louis Jacobs, The Jewish Religion: A Companion (New York: Oxford University Press, 1995), 545, and Watson E. Mills and Roger Aubrey Bullard, Mercer Dictionary of the Bible (Macon, GA: Mercer University Press, 1990), 889.

4 George Buchanan Gray, "Divine Names" in *Encyclopaedia Biblica,* Vol. 3, eds. T.K. Cheyne and J. Sutherland Black (London: Black, 1899), 3320.

5 David Noel Freedman et al., "יהוה YHWH," *in Theological Dictionary of the Old Testament,* ed. G.J. Botterweck and H. Ringgren, Trns. J.T. Willis, G.W. Bromiley and D.E. Green, Vol.5 (Grand Rapids, Michigan: Eerdsman, 1974), 500.

6 William Albright, *From the Stone Age to Christianity: Monotheism and the Historical Process* (2nd edition; New York: Doubleday Anchor Book, 1957), 15.

7 David Noel Freedman, "Divine names and Titles in early Hebrew Poetry," in *Magnalia Dei: The Mighty Acts of God, Essays on the Bible and Archeology in Memory of G. Ernest Wright,* eds. Frank Moore Cross et al. (New York: Doubleday, 1979), 55.

the famous 'I AM' interaction with Moses (Ex. 3) and references the fact that God has always existed and will always exist. God wants to have a relationship with His people, and so He is giving them permission to call Him by a personal name rather than by His formal name.

The use of the designation YHWH in the Bible shows no recognition of the etymology of the term, and there is no indication in the Hebrew Bible of a theology being built around the meaning of the name. Nevertheless, these theories on the etymology of the term YHWH are deceptive, even if the original meaning of the name is definitely identified; there is still no assurance that the Israelites understood the name correctly.

ELOHIM

The Hebrew Bible uses three related words for 'God'- namely, *El, Eloha*, and *Elohim*.[8] In general, the words are usually translated as God and usually are treated as having the same meaning. There is no commonly accepted etymological explanation of the meaning of the term Elohim.[9] Grammatically, the form ◌ִהלֹאֱ ים contains the plural ending- im.[10] The function of Elohim as a true plural (gods) is reflected in several biblical texts (Ex. 12:12, 'all the gods of Egypt'). One of the more prominent features of the Hebrew Bible is the use of this plural form in order to designate the one true God of Israel. Anderson view this as a plural of majesty as equivalent to 'deity' or 'godhead'[11] as Elohim includes all gods; the fullness of deity is comprehended in him. This 'plural of

---

8 Helmer Ringgren, ◌ִהלֹאֱ ים *elohim*, in *Theological Dictionary of the Old Testament*: Vol. 1, eds., G. Johannes Botterweck and Helmer Ringgren (Grand Rapids, Michigan: Eerdmans, 1974), 185.

9 John McKenzie, "Aspects of Old Testament Theology" in *New Jerome Biblical Commentary*, eds. Raymond Edward Brown, Joseph A. Fitzmyer, and Roland E. Murphy (Englewood Cliffs, NJ: Prentice-Hall, 1990), 1285.

10 Martin Rose, "Names of God in the Old Testament", in *Anchor Bible Dictionary*, Vol. 4, ed. David Noel Freedman, (New York, 1992), 1006.

11 Bernhard Anderson, "God, names of" in *The Interpreter's Dictionary of the Bible,* Vol. 2, ed. G.A. Buttrick (New York: Abindon Press, 1962), 413.

majesty', according to Anderson and Eichrodt[12] did not first arise in Israelite tradition on the contrary; this is an ancient pre-Israelite expression, which was used in Babylon and Canaan. Anderson gives the example how the Akkadians used the plural word *ilanu* 'gods' in homage to a particular god, such as the moon god Sin, to express the worshipper's view that he is the highest or greatest God, in whom the entire Pantheon is represented.[13] In this way in the Bible when Yahweh is termed Elohim, He is 'God of gods', 'The highest God', 'quintessence of all divine powers', 'the only God who represents the divine in a comprehensive and absolute way.'[14] Elohim as a designation of YHWH characterized him as the absolute God. Yahweh is inherently distinct and superior to all other gods. Yahweh is an elohim (a god), but no other elohim (gods) are Yahweh.

There are other beings in the Old Testament that are called elohim besides Yahweh. Demons (Deut. 32:17)[15] and the spirits of the human dead (1 Sam. 28:13) are also called elohim in the Hebrew text. Angels (Gen. 35:7) may also be called elohim.

12 Walter Eichrodt, *Theology of the Old Testament* (London: SCM Press, 1961), 185.

13 Anderson, "God, names of"..., 413.

14 Rose, "Names of God in the Old Testament"..., 1006.

15 In Deut. 32, Moses is rehearsing how Israel sinned during their wilderness trek by worshipping other gods. In verse 17 we read: "They sacrificed to demons, not God, to deities (elohim) they had never known, to new ones recently arrived, and whom your ancestors had not feared." The important observation is that the Israelites sacrificed to demons, and those recipients of the sacrifices are also called gods (elohim).

The other names of God are Adonai,[16] Qanna,[17] El Shaddai,[18] El Elyon,[19] El Olam,[20] Jehovah Rapha,[21] Jehovah

---

16 It is the verbal parallel to Yahweh. *Adonai* is plural, the singular is *adon*. In reference to God the plural *Adonai* is used. When the singular *adon* is used, it usually refers to a human Lord. *Adon* is used 215 times to refer to men. Occasionally, in Scripture and predominantly in the Psalms, the singular *adon* is used to refer to God as well. Sometimes, *Adonai* was used as a substitute for Yahweh. *Adonai* can be translated literally as "my Lords". In the Old Testament it occurs 434 times. It is first used in Gen. 15:2. (Ernst Jenni, "adon", in Theological Lexicon of the Old Testament, trs. Mark Biddle Vol. 1 Peabody, 26).

17 It is translated as "Jealous", or "envy". The fundamental meaning relates to a marriage relationship. God is depicted as Israel's husband; He is a jealous God, wanting all our praise for Himself and no one else (Ex. 34:14). (Frank Moore Cross, Canaanite Myth and Hebrew Epic: Essays in the History of the Religion of Israel, Cambridge: Harvard University Press, 1973, 52-60).

18 *El* is another name that is translated as "God" and can be used in conjunction with other words to designate various aspects of God's character. *Shad* means "breast" in Hebrew (some other scholars believe that the name is derived from an Akkadian word *Sadu*, meaning "mountain", suggesting strength and power). This refers to God completely nourishing, satisfying, and supplying His people with all their needs as a mother would her child. Connected with the word for God, *El,* it denotes a God who freely gives nourishment and blessing, He is our sustainer. In the Old Testament it occurs 7 times. It is first used in Gen. 17:1. (Maire Byrne, The names of God in Judaism, Christianity, and Islam: A Basis for interfaith Dialogue, New York: Continuum International Publishing Group, 2011, 26).

19 *Elyon* literally means "Most High" and is used both adjectivally and substantively throughout the Old Testament. It expresses the extreme sovereignty and majesty of God and His highest preeminence. When the two words are combined - *El Elyon* - it can be translated as "the most exalted God." In the Old Testament it occurs 28 times. It occurs 19 times in Psalms. It is first used in Gen. 14:18. (Byrne, The names of God in Judaism, Christianity, and Islam…)

20 *Olam* derives from the root word *lam* (which means "eternity"). *Olam* literally means "forever," "eternity," or "everlasting". When the two words are combined it can be translated as "The Eternal God". (Byrne, The names of God in Judaism, Christianity, and Islam…)

21 *Jehovah* is translated as "The Existing One" or "Lord." The chief meaning of *Jehovah* is derived from the Hebrew word *Havah* meaning "to be" or "to exist." It also suggests "to become" or specifically "to become known"

Mekoddishkem,[22] Jehovah Jireh,[23] Jehovah Shalom,[24] Jehovah Sabaoth,[25] and Jehovah Tsidkenu.[26]

The Understanding of God

As been mentioned in the introduction, human understanding of God is limited by the finite abilities that human has been created

---

- this denotes a God who reveals Himself unceasingly. *Rapha* means "to restore", "to heal" or "to make healthful" in Hebrew. When the two words are combined - *Jehovah Rapha* - it can be translated as "Jehovah Who Heals." The great physician who heals the physical and emotional needs of His people. (David Cunningham, "On translating the divine name" in Theological Studies 56 (1995): 424).

22 *Mekoddishkem* derives from the Hebrew word *qadash* meaning "sanctify," "holy" or "dedicate". Sanctification is the separation of an object or person to the dedication of the Holy. When the two words are combined - *Jehovah Mekoddishkem* - it can be translated as "The Lord who sets you apart". In the Old Testament it occurs only 2 times (Ex. 31:13; Lev.20:8). (Byrne, The names of God in Judaism, Christianity, and Islam…)

23 *Jehovah-Jireh* is a symbolic name given to Mount Moriah by Abraham to memorialize the intercession of God in the sacrifice of Isaac by providing a substitute for the imminent sacrifice of his son. In the Old Testament it occurs only once in Gen. 22:14. It simply means The Lord will provide. (Byrne, The names of God in Judaism, Christianity, and Islam…)

24 Shalom is a derivative of *shalem* (which means "be complete" or "sound") *Shalom* is translated as "peace" or "absence from strife." *Jehovah-Shalom* is the name of an altar built by Gideon in Ophrah. It means The Lord is peace. In the Old Testament *Jehovah-Shalom* occurs only once in Jdg.6:24. (Byrne, The names of God in Judaism, Christianity, and Islam…)

25 *Sabaoth* means "armies" or "hosts." *Jehovah Sabaoth* can be translated as "The Lord of Armies" (1 Sam 1:3). This name denotes His universal sovereignty over every army, both spiritual and earthly. The Lord of Hosts is the king of all heaven and earth. *Jehovah* and *Elohim* occur with *Sabaoth* over 285 times. It is most frequently used in Jeremiah and Isaiah. It is first used in 1 Sam. 1:3. (E. Theodore Mullan, "Hosts, host of heaven" in *Anchor Bible Dictionary*, vol. 3, ed. David Noel Freedman, 301).

26 *Tsidkenu* is derived from *tsedek* which means righteous, to be straight or to be stiff in Hebrew. When the two words are combined, i.e., *Jehovah Tsidkenu* it is translated as "The Lord Who is our Righteousness". In the Old Testament it occur only two times, i.e., in Jer. 23:6; 33:16. (Byrne, The names of God in Judaism, Christianity, and Islam…)

with. Our knowledge of God cannot be exhaustive, for the finite is attempting to understand the Infinite who has revealed Himself. If we had an infinite and completely comprehensive understanding of God, we too, would be God, having omniscience. God ever remains somewhat of an inexplicable 'mystery' to the finite understanding of human. The Bible makes no attempt to prove that God exists. Rather, the universe is the affidavit of his existence. God has revealed Himself to humanity through His book, the Bible. By reading and studying His book, we learn who He is, how He responds, and how He revealed Himself to us.

God can only be known to the extent that He reveals Himself. "No one has seen God at any time", but God has revealed Himself in His natural creation (Rom. 1:20), as a Personal God to His people (Ex. 3:14), and subsequently revealed Himself supernaturally in the incarnation of His Son, Jesus Christ (Jn. 1:14; 14:9). Our understanding of God is not a result of independent human reasoning having set out to find God and figure Him out. Our knowledge of God comes only by means of, and must be derived out of, His own Self-revelation. We must allow God to determine our understanding of Himself, and that by His own Self-revelation.

In this attempt to develop 'a Christian understanding of God' there are two presuppositional premises that will be used to format our thinking. They are;[27] *What God is, only God is. God does what He does, because He is who He is.*

What God is, only God is.

This means that God stands alone as Who He *is*. "What God *is*, only God *is*," is expressed equivalently as "Who God *is*; only God *is*."[28] By using the pronoun 'what', it does not imply that God is an impersonal being. We, the personal beings who make this inquiry into a Christian understanding of God, cannot entertain the illogic

27 James, A. Fowler, *The Etiology of Creation* (Fallbrook: CIY Publishing, 1991), 67.

28 Notice that the premise has already been expanded by using the personal pronoun, "Who."

of the personal derived from the impersonal, the living derived from the non-living, or something derived out of nothing.[29]

The Bible begins, "*In the beginning God* (the living, personal God) created…" (Gen. 1:1) all things – all things apart from Himself and except Himself, for He Himself is Self-existent (not self-created or self-caused, but self-existent). The Bible presupposes the existence of God, and does not attempt to prove God's existence. God is the Self-existent, Creator God-and "what God *is*, only God *is*." God, the Self-existent Creator, must be regarded as distinct from the creation that He, the Creator God, created.[30]

The extension of this premise must be applied to all of the attributes of God. "What God *is*, only God *is*." There have been long attempted to differentiate between the 'non-transferable attributes' of God and the 'transferable attributes' of God. Such attributes as omnipresence, omnipotence and omniscience have been regarded as God-only attributes which are non-transferable to human or the created order. Attributes such as "God *is* Good", "God *is* Holy", and "God *is* Love" have been regarded as character qualities of God that are transferable to human. The problem with this interpretation is that the attributes of God are not 'properties' or 'features' which God *has* as transferable commodities. The attributes of God are what God *is* in Himself, and are thus non-transferable, for "what God *is,* only God *is*." Anytime we attempt to attribute an attribute of God to anything or anyone else, we ever so subtly deify, or attribute an attribute of deity, to that other thing or person.

God is absolutely, intrinsically, inherently, self-existently Good, Holy, and Love, and the source of all goodness, holiness and love within His creation. Whenever His character is expressed within His creation, it is necessarily He expressing such. When Christians are referred to as 'holy ones' or 'saints', it is only

29 C.S. Lewis, *Mere Christianity* (New York: Macmillan Publishing, 1978), 102.

30 Colin E. Gunton, *The Promise of Trinitarian Theology* (Edinburgh: T & T Clark, 1995), 164.

because God, in Christ, the Holy One (Acts 3:14) is present and indwelling that individual, comprising the basis of their spiritual identity.

Such a derived identity allows for the derived expression of God's holy character in the behaviour of the Christian. Holiness is intrinsic to and inherent in God alone.[31]

God does what He does, because He is who He is.

The second presupposition premise for a Christian understanding of God is just as important as the first. "God *does* what He *does*, because He *is* Who He *is*". A Christian understanding of God must commence with who God *is*, and then proceed to what God *does*.

Otherwise God's being is established by His doing, and God is nothing more than a mechanical and functional principle of action that can be proceduralized for useful purposes. Christian theology must commence with the character of God, Who God *is*, recognizing such from God's own Self-revelation. From the basis of His own character, God conducts Himself in absolute consistency with who He *is*. God *does* what He *does*, because He *is* Who He *is* (Ex. 3:13-14).[32]

God's being is the basis of His doing, and not *vice versa*. God's character is always expressed in His actions. There is no divine action that is not empowered by and expressive of His own divine Being. The very Being of God cannot be separated or detached from anything God does. God does not employ a formula, a principle, or a law to accomplish what He seeks to do. He did not create, for example, by utilizing a "spiritual law of speaking a word of faith". Rather, God created out of Himself, His action being incorporative with the entirety of His Being.[33] In so creating out of Himself, He could still create that which was not

---

31 J.I. Packer, *Knowing God* (London: Hodder and Stoughton, 1973), 15.

32 Fowler, *Towards a Christian Understanding of God* (Fallbrook: CIY Publishing, 2002), 21.

33 Geoffrey H. Parke Taylor, *YHWH: The Divine Name in the Bible* (Waterloo: Wilfrid Laurier University Press, 1975), 11.

Himself, and thus retaining the important distinction between the Creator and the creation.

The Being of God is never passive, but always active. God always acts out of His own Being. He acts in accord with Who He is, i.e., consistent with His own character. For God *is* faithful and He cannot deny Himself.[34] He cannot deny Who He *is* by acting contrary to Who He *is*. God *is* in His essential Being, absolute Truth, and He cannot act contrary to His character. His activity will always express His Being. "God *does* what He *does*, only because He *is* Who He *is*."[35] God express Himself in many ways but the best way in which He communicates human being is through His perfect Love which we will see below.

The Understanding of God's Love (*Hesed*)

God's Love has been depicted throughout the Old Testament. The heart of Yahweh has been to reach all people so they can experience His divine love. The presenter will use the word *Hesed*[36] in defining or understanding God's love. Indeed, *hesed* is difficult to translate. No single word in English captures its meanings. Translators use words like 'kindness', 'loving-kindness', 'mercy', 'loyalty' and 'steadfast love. According to the BDB, *hesed* means goodness or kindness.[37]*Hesed* is one of the richest, most powerful words in the Old Testament. It is not a 'mood'. *Hesed* is not primarily something people 'feel'. It is something people 'do' for other people who have no claim on them. Love is something we do, not primarily something we feel. *Hesed* is a quality of life that should characterize those who know God.

---

34 The Bible states that "with God, nothing is impossible" (Lk.1:37), but it turns right around and says, "it is impossible for God to lie" (Heb. 6:18). Why can God not lie? Because God "cannot deny Himself."

35 Raymond Abba, "The divine name YHWH", in *Journal of Biblical Literature*, 80 (1961), 326.

36 Hereafter hesed or love will be interchangeably used.

37 F. Brown, S. Driver, C. Briggs, *The Brown-Driver-Briggs Hebrew-English Lexicon* (Mass: Hendrickson, 2005), 338.

Hesed has both God and human as its subject. When man is the subject of *hesed*, the word usually describes the person's kindness or loyalty to another, 2 Sam. 9:7. Only rarely is the term applied explicitly to human affection or fidelity toward God (Jer. 2:2). *Hesed* is not only exercised toward family and relatives, but also to friends, guests, masters and servants. Hos. 6:6 states that God desires *hesed* and not sacrifice. God's *hesed* is offered to His people, who need redemption from sin, enemies and troubles. A recurrent refrain describing God's nature is 'abounding/ plenteous' in *hesed* (Ex 34:6; Neh. 9:17; Ps 103:8; Jonah 4:2). The entire history of Yahweh's covenantal relationship with Israel can be summarized in terms of *hesed.* It is the one permanent element in the flux of covenantal history. Even the Creation is a result of God's *hesed* (Ps 136:5-9). His love lasts for a 'thousand generations' (Dt. 7:9; Ex 20:6).[38]

God's *hesed* is not bound by the covenant itself, and though human may prove unfaithful to this relationship, God's *hesed* is everlasting (Isa 54:8).[39] Since it is a quality of God, hesed should also characterize His people; therefore it is called for in them (Mic 6:8; Zech 7:9; Ho 4:1; 12:6). On their part it is loyalty to His covenant expressed in obedience and acts of mercy and compassion toward their fellows. It is a life-long love that is richer and deeper than English has ever conceived of- *hesed.* Based in a covenantal relationship, *hesed* is a steadfast, rock-solid faithfulness that endures to eternity. (Isa. 54:10). *Hesed* is to love as God loves. When God's presence passed by Moses on Mt. Sinai and revealed his very essence, God proclaimed his great *hesed.* (Exo. 34:6). John Oswalt describes it this way:

> The word *hesed*...(is) the descriptor par excellence of God in the Old Testament. The word speaks of a completely undeserved kindness and generosity done by a person who is in a position of power. This was the Israelites' experience

38 W. E. Vine, *Vine's Complete Expository Dictionary of Old and New Testament Words* (Nelson, 1996), 105.

39 Eugene Petersen, *The Message* (Colorado Springs: NavPress Publishing Group, 1993), 69.

> of God. He revealed himself to them when they were not looking for him, and he kept his covenant with them long after their persistent breaking of it had destroyed any reason for his continued keeping of it..., Unlike humans, this deity was not fickle, undependable, self-serving, and grasping. Instead he was faithful, true, upright and generous always.[40]

In fact, the entire world is the stage for the demonstration of Yahweh's *hesed*.[41] He has indeed filled the whole earth with His love. *Hesed* shapes not only the relationship of Yahweh with human beings, but also that of human beings among themselves. Albrecht Ritschl (1822-1889) did not like the notion of a wrathful God. Ritschl concluded, "The concept of God's wrath has no religious value for the Christian". So he reinterpreted the meaning of wrath. Wrath is the logical consequence of God's absence, and not God's attitude toward sin and evil. God is above getting angry. God's love towards each one of us is unconditional.[42]

God's *hesed* is relational; it is always directed toward other persons – not ideas, principles, theories or things. It is always *other*-oriented, giving oneself for the other. God reached out in *hesed* to fallen humanity – simply because He is Love. And such *hesed* is not conditioned by the condition of the object of His Love; it is not predicated on the loveableness of the object. God loved, and loves the unlovely. The story of Hosea illustrates that God loves those who do not even appreciate His love and even reject His love.[43]

God is intrinsic to Who He *is*. He always gives Himself for others. He always acts out of His being of *hesed*. This *hesed* is not

---

40 John Oswalt, *The Bible among the Myths* (Grand Rapids, Michigan: Zondervan, 2009), 7.

41 G. Johannes Botterweck, Helmer Ringgren, *Theological Dictionary of the Old Testament* (Grand Rapids, Eerdmans, 1986), 62.

42 Ritschl, Albrecht, *The Christian Doctrine of Justification and Reconciliation: The Positive Development of the Doctrine*, trs. H.R. Mackintosh and A.B. Macaulay (Edinburgh: T. & T. Clark, 1902), 72.

43 D.A. Carson, *For the Love of God,* Vol.1 (Crossway Books Publishers, 1998), 54.

just a sentiment or subjective feeling. It is not an idealistic virtue or moral principle. It is not passive or theoretical.[44] The *hesed* of God is always extending to others by giving Himself completely for their highest good.

Conclusion

In the theology of the name of God, the revelation of the name YHWH to Israel through Moses represented a new and fuller revelation of the personal reality of YHWH. For the people of Israel know God by this name and no further qualification or definition is needed. He is known for what He is (as the living God) and by what He does (in terms of showing His *hesed* in action through creating, saving, redeeming, and so forth). It is through his manifestation that YHWH became known, with each appearance, some more detail of his character and plan is revealed.

Normally, *hesed* describes something that happens within an existing relationship, whether between two human beings or between God and human. In human relationships, *hesed* implies loving our neighbour, not merely in terms of warm emotional feelings but in acts of love and service that we owe to the other person. God's people are to do justly, to love *hesed*, and to walk humbly with their God (Mic. 6:8).

God's *hesed* is an inclusive world. It is for the world. Not simply the respectable, religious, lovable parts of the world but the world in to. It is a cosmic love that loves the cosmos to death and in so doing saves it. Only when the *hesed* of God is express within the people, then we will see the loving, interpersonal community that God intends. When "faith is working through love", our receptivity to the activity of God's love, then there will be no thought of what we get out of it, no thought of who gets the credit, no thought of reciprocity, and no thought of who is in control. The God, who is Love, wants to manifest His character of *hesed* in our behaviour, individually and collectively.

The fullness of the Lord's *hesed* is seen in the cross; there the true *hesed*, Jesus Christ Himself- the one who was truly loyal

44 A nice idea about being nice to nice people.

to the Lord and to His neighbor in every aspect of life-was treated as the covenant breaker and cursed for sin so that we who are unfaithful might be clothed in His faithfulness and thus redeemed. In this way, God's original covenant purpose to have a people for His praise was faithfully accomplished.

The Old Testament understanding is that the Creator God is good, and "what God is, only God is." Though the opposite of good, i.e., evil, has come into the world and into human, God has overcome that evil in the death of His Son, Jesus Christ because of His *hesed* and God's intent is to restore His character of *hesed* to His creation. Thus, the functional understanding of God will help each individual in living out His *hesed* and bring loving interpersonal relationships within the entire human race.

2

Peacemaking and Dialogue in the History of Christianity

Woba James[1]

Introduction

Down through the centuries, the Church had to face the challenge of conflicts, dissensions and trying issues that call for her active yet critical involvement in peacemaking and dialogue within itself as well as with the society.

To begin with, few Bible verses can be recalled regarding peace. These are some of the classic biblical passages on peace. "Peace I leave with you; my peace I give you. I do not give to you as the world gives. Do not let your hearts be troubled and do not be afraid." (Jn 14:27). "Come to me, all you who are weary and burdened, and I will give you rest. Take my yoke upon you and learn from me, for I am gentle and humble in heart, and you will find rest for your souls. For my yoke is easy and my burden is light." (Mt 11:28-30). "For God is not a God of disorder but of peace." (1 Cor 14:33). "May the God of hope fill you with all joy and peace as you trust in him, so that you may overflow with hope by the power of the Holy Spirit." (Ro 15:13).

---

1 Rev. Dr. Woba James is an Associate Professor and HoD of History of Christianity at Eastern Theological College, Jorhat, Assam.

What is Peacemaking?

What do we understand by 'peacemaking'? There is no simple or no 'one' definite definition for 'peacemaking' which could be applicable for all situations and contexts. It is variegated in content and approach and at/for different issues and situations. It could very well be any or every of the following;

- High-level diplomats working out a regional plan for addressing conflicts in the world today.
- Civil society organizations bringing religious leaders together to dialogue in a conflict zone.
- Different groups working together across the lines of conflict in different corners of the world to deliver humanitarian aid to families in conflict region.
- Leaders of different religious groups coming together to bring harmony to conflicted regions, etc.

Yes, peacemaking could be all of these and even more! The questions connected to peacemaking are often debated among policymakers. Is conflict something that should be managed, mitigated, negotiated, mediated, resolved, prevented or transformed? Is peacemaking something to be kept, made or built? These questions emerge time and again. We need to understand that peacemaking is a process of strengthening a society's or a community's capacity to handle or manage conflict in peaceful ways. Conflict is natural in society and can have the potentiality for positive change, however, if it is not properly managed, it can lead to violence and destruction. Hence, peacemaking implies the use of cooperative, constructive processes to resolve human conflicts, restoring and strengthening relationships.

What is Dialogue?

According to Paulo Freire, "dialogue is the encounter between men, mediated by the world, in order to name the world."[2] He further elaborates saying, "dialogue is a written or

2 Paulo Freire, *Pedagogy of the Oppressed* (Oxford: Penguin Publisher, 1996), 34.

spoken conversational exchange between two or more people, and a literary and theatrical form that depicts such an exchange."[3] According to William Isaacs, "dialogue is the art of thinking together and is a conversation with a centre and not with sides. It is a way of taking the energy of our differences and channelling it toward something that has never been created before. It lifts us out of polarization and into a greater common sense, and is thereby a means for accessing the intelligence and coordinated power of groups of people."[4] Therefore in this paper, dialogue is being taken into consideration as dialogue between the state and the church and between the Christians themselves.

A Brief Survey of Peacemaking and Dialogue in the History of the Church

Peacemaking and Dialogue till 600 A.D.

Peace has always been among humanity's highest values. Many Christians suspect the Old Testament God as a God who is violent, warlike, sometimes cruel, whereas in the New Testament, God is understood as a God who is gentle and compassionate, patient, understanding, loving and a caring God. Peace was considered as the most important aspect of the Church since the foundation of the history of Christianity is based on the very message of peace. However, disputes, conflicts, rivalries, struggles and even group confrontations have existed since the birth of humankind, and also, wars have been taking place since the existence of nations. Peace therefore is the needed conceptual ideal in the midst of such peace-less situations. In the Old Testament accounts, especially in Genesis 25-35, one gathers that the god/protector of the clan is initiator for peacemaking and dialogue for harmonious and peaceful living among the people. In this world, it is not creating war that makes a person great but people who make peace. The

---

3 *Ibid*, 57.

4 Cf. William Isaacs, *Dialogue: The Art of Thinking Together* (New York: Crown Publishing, 2008), 19.

Bible portrayed it through the very life of Jesus Christ, standing in between the Holy God and the fallen creatures (John 3:16).[5]

Christ implanted in the minds of His followers the idea of the peaceful kingdom of God. "Seek ye first the kingdom of God and His righteousness and all these things shall be added unto you" (Mt 6:33). They did seek the kingdom of God and His righteousness and the church grew in strength, love and in faith. As far as history is concerned, the relation between the Church and the State was cordial till A.D. 64. According to church father Tertullian, the peacemaking and dialogue that took place in the history of the (early) church was where Emperor Tiberius (14-37 A.D.) consulted and suggested that Christianity should be considered as one of the imperial religions.[6] However, that peacemaking between the Church and the State was broken down with the emergence of the severe conflicts between the Roman Emperor and Christian community in 64 A.D. Again, peacemaking and dialogue took place between the Church and State around 68-69 A.D. sometime during the reigns of emperors Vespasian (68-79 A.D.) and Titus (79-81 A.D.).[7] As the church existed within the Roman world, different church leaders tried their best to build peace between them and the then rulers. According to church father Eusebius, during the time of Emperor Domitian (81-96 A.D.) all the peace efforts were once again torn down and Christians were persecuted in almost the entire continent of the Roman world.[8] In many cases, it was not due to the sole intention of the Emperor but mostly with the advices and influences of his procurators and governors that break the peaceful situations between the Empire and Christianity.

During the 2nd and the 3rd centuries, peacemaking and dialogue between the church and the State, we see a continuous

5 Cf. Cullean, J. Ayer, *A Source Book for Ancient Church History* (New York: Charles Scribers, 1941), 26. (Hereafter cited as Ayer, *Ancient Church History*).

6 Cf. Arbesmann, Rudolph, Trans., *Tertullian Apologetical Works and Minucius Felix Oclavius* (Washington: The Catholic University Press, 1962), 56.

7 Cf. Eusebius, *Ecclesiastical History* (London: ISPCK, 1927), 59.

8 Cf. *Nicene and Post Nicene Fathers,* Vol. 1, 34.

struggle to establish the state of peace within the church. The declaration of Christianity as an illegal religion within the Roman Empire made it impossible to develop a peaceful co-existence with the then world. However, the church was able to make peace within the Roman world during the time of Emperor Trajan 98 A.D. to Antonius Pius 161 A.D.[9] Church fathers like Tertullian and Justin Martyr and several others took peacemaking and dialogue initiatives during these centuries in spite of all the conflicts in the then world. It was said that during the reigns of Septimius Severus (193-221 A.D.) and Alexander Severus (222-235 A.D.), there was a peaceful atmosphere in the history of the church and state. According to church father Eusebius, Emperor Philip (244-249 A.D.) was a Christian emperor and peace was maintained during his reign.[10]

Peacemaking and dialogue in the church and state came under a severe blow during the middle of the 3rd century again with the reign of Emperor Decius (249-251 A.D.) who ordered not to have any association with the church and it was followed till 313 A.D., but with the Edict of Milan in 313 A.D. where Christianity came to be proclaimed a legit religion, peacemaking and dialogue initiatives taken by several church leaders came to be realized at last. Peacemaking and dialogue initiatives were not taken by the church leaders alone but also with the Emperors' initiatives sometimes.[11] With the Edict of Milan in 313 A.D. the whole Christian church came to enjoy the peaceful atmosphere. With the coming of Emperor Constantine, the church continued to grow and even spread to almost all parts of the world.

On the other hand, with the Edict of Milan, there also came in the history of the church two distinctive divisions of the church, i.e., Western Christianity and Eastern Christianity. Peacemaking and dialogue initiatives came from the Emperors themselves in order to bring together these two churches but failed to achieve the goal. Under the signature of Emperor Constantine, the Council of

---

9 Eusebius, *Ecclesiastical History* (London: ISPCK, 1927), 90.

10 *Ibid*, 109.

11 Cf. *Nicene and Post Nicene Fathers*, Vol. 1, 56.

Nicaea was held in 325 A.D. but even that council could not bring them together.[12] This was followed by several initiatives from the emperors and bishops to reconcile yet all of these peace efforts failed.[13] Several councils were called for reconciliation between these two groups of Christianity. In addition, we should understand that all these peacemaking and dialogue were also disturbed by theological controversies which resulted in wider differences between the Eastern Christianity and Western Christianity.

Peacemaking till the Reformation

With the coming of the power of the barbarian tribes that overtook the Roman Empire during the end of the 5th century, the very existence of the Western Church was questioned. Several years of peaceful existence was confronted again with paganism, heretical teachings, invasions, racial diversity and political instability in the history of the world. All these threaten the very peaceful situation of the church and the state. With the fading of the Roman power, gradually the bishops became more effective in peacemaking in the church and state.[14] During the 6th century, Bishop Gregory the Great was instrumental in peacemaking and dialogue between the Church and the then State.[15] It was under his leadership along with the bishops that peace was maintained within the European Church during the medieval period.

The rivalry between the Eastern Christianity and Western Christianity continued to exist even after several councils and resolutions. Though the Roman power came to an end in the Western world, in the Eastern world it continued to survive for many more centuries.[16] All efforts to reconcile these two churches collapsed with the violent quarrel that broke out between Patriarch

12 Eusebius, *Ecclesiastical History* (London: ISPCK, 1927), 120.

13 Cf. *Nicene and Post Nicene Fathers,* Vol. 1, 68.

14 Cf. Walter Wink, *Engaging the Powers: Discernment and Resistance in a World of Domination* (Minneapolis: Fortress Press, 1992), 90.

15 Cf. Ayer, *Ancient Church History,* 37.

16 Cf. Arthur Carr, *Church and the Roman Empire* (London: Longmanns Gree & Co., 1895), 38.

Cerularius and the envoys of Pope Leo Xin 1054. Pope's legate Cardinal Humbert ex-communicated Cerularius, who in turn, ex-communicated the Western legates.[17] With this final event, peacemaking and dialogue between the West and East came to an end. However, that does not completely stop the peace efforts as different individuals and groups continued to work to mend the rift between these two churches and state. It resulted in the two of the most popular peacemaking and dialogue initiative attempts namely, the Council of Lyon (1274 A.D.) and the Council of Florence (1439 A.D.). Yet again, the point of no hope for peace between the Western Christianity and the Eastern Christianity came in 1484 when the Council of Constantinople rejected the peacemaking and dialogue initiatives of the Council of Florence.

Peacemaking and dialogue in the history of the church also suffered with the outbreak of Muslims in the east. The conflict between Islam and Christianity served a severe setback for the church in the East. Meanwhile, in the 11th century, European church began several holy crusades to recapture the Holy Land from the Muslims that led to total failure of peacemaking and dialogue in the history of the church. Theologians like Peter Abelard, Peter Lombard, Thomas Aquinas, Augustine of Hippo, Latin Averorists, Gregory Palamas and more in the later period such as Francis of Assisi, Dominic de Guzman, John Wycliffe, Czech John Huss, etc., all took peacemaking and dialogue as a serious cause for the furthering of the church. They all advocated that the church need to maintain peaceful living with the state without corruption as Christ was corrupt less. Peacemaking and dialogue initiatives during these centuries especially in the Eastern Church came to an end with the collapse of the Byzantine Empire in 1453 A.D. under the power of the Muslims.

Peacemaking in the Post-Reformation

In the Post reformation era, peacemaking and dialogue initiative of the church revealed series of changes that took place in the

17 Cf. Huizinga Johan, *Erasmus and the Age of Reformation* (New York: Harper, 1957), 100-101.

Western Christianity. 16th century was the century of reformation. The 17th century was dominated by Counter Reformation directed principally by the Jesuits. The church at these times was in very weak form. Several bishops and church leaders were even said to have stopped going to their churches. The services were perfunctory, without any interest, churches were neglected, and everywhere there was a sign of apathy or indifference.[18] The educated and affluent classes on the whole remained detached from the church. The working classes were in great poverty, often in destitution and for all practical purposes they were outside the church. The church had very much neglected the spiritual and peacemaking aspects of the people and the society. Nevertheless, there were people who lived and aspired to have peace among the Christians as well as between the church and state.

In the early sixteenth century, the western world had a single official religion and that was Catholicism, and the head of the Church was the Pope in Rome. Catholic liturgy and the Bible were in Latin, which only few lay people understood.[19] In Germany in November 1517, Martin Luther protested against corruption in the Catholic Church and began a protest movement that came to be known as the Reformation. The European Reformation promoted two central ideas;

1) sola scriptura: only the Scriptures have religious authority and not Church clerics or traditions.
2) sola fide: only the faith of the individual (not good works or rituals) can affect his or her salvation.[20]

With the rise of the Reformation, serious conflicts among the Christians took place. The conflicts and tensions were even strengthened by the rise of nations and national feeling which began to break the western world. Religious persecutions and

18 Cf. John Bossy, *Peace in the Post-Reformation* (Oxford: Cambridge University Press, 1998), 36.

19 Euan Cameron, *The European Reformation* (Oxford and New York, 1991), 76.

20 Cf. Martin Luther, *The Large Catechism,* trans. by Robert H. Fisher (Philadelphia: Fortress, 1959), 2-3.

even war broke out between Roman Catholic and Protestant forces. Peacemaking and dialogue attempts were made to bring peace between the warring Roman Catholics and the Protestants.[21] Therefore, in 1648 the Peace of Westphalia,[22] the boundaries

21 Erasmus, "The Complaint of Peace", *The Essential Erasmus*, ed. John Dolan (New York: Continuum, 1990), 177.

22 The Westphalia area of north-western Germany gave its name to the treaty that ended the Thirty Years' War, one of the most destructive conflicts in the history of Europe. The war or series of connected wars began in 1618, when the Austrian Habsburgs tried to impose Roman Catholicism on their Protestant subjects in Bohemia. It pitted Protestant against Catholic, the Holy Roman Empire against France, the German princes and princelings against the emperor and each other, and France against the Habsburgs of Spain. The Swedes, the Danes, the Poles, the Russians, the Dutch and the Swiss were all dragged in or dived in. Commercial interests and rivalries played a part, as did religion and power politics. Among famous commanders involved were Marshal Turenne and the Prince de Condé for France, Wallenstein for the Empire and Tilly for the Catholic League, and there was an able Bavarian general curiously named Franz von Mercy. Others to play a part ranged from the Winter King of Bohemia to the emperors Ferdinand II and Ferdinand III, Bethlen Gabor of Transylvania, Christian IV of Denmark, Gustavus II Adolphus and Queen Christina of Sweden, the Great Elector of Brandenburg, Philip IV of Spain and his brother the Cardinal-Infante, Louis XIII of France, Cardinals Richelieu and Mazarin and several popes. Gustavus Adolphus was shot in the head and killed at the battle of Lutzen in 1632. The increasingly crazed Wallenstein, who grew so sensitive to noise that he had all the dogs, cats and cockerels killed in every town he came to, was murdered by an English captain in 1634. Still the fighting went on. The peace conference to end the war opened in Münster and Osnabrück in December 1644. It involved no fewer than 194 states, from the biggest to the smallest, represented by 179 plenipotentiaries. There were thousands of ancillary diplomats and support staff, who had to be given housing, fed and watered, and they did themselves well for close to four years, despite famine in the country around. Presiding over the conference were the Papal Nuncio, Fabio Chigi (the future Pope Alexander VII), and the Venetian ambassador. The first six months were spent arguing about who was to sit where and who was to go into a room ahead of whom. The principal French and Spanish envoys never managed to meet at all because the correct protocol could not be agreed. A special postal system handled reams of letters between the envoys and their principals at a time when it took ten days or more to send a communication from Münster to Paris or Vienna and twenty days or more to Stockholm or Madrid. Slowly deals

between the Roman and Protestant Christian were drawn. Newer forms of separation soon appeared among the Protestants with the emergence of Anabaptists,[23] a number of independent mystical and spiritual thinkers, theological controversies and separatist groups. To build peace among those protestant groups was also a difficult task for the church.[24] Though several peacemaking and dialogue initiatives took place, conflicts grew into bigger tensions as evidenced in the history of the church.

Peacemaking and Dialogue between the Western Christianity and Eastern Christianity till 19th Century

As per the records of the Church History, for many centuries, the Eastern Christianity and the Western Christianity lived in almost complete separation from one another. Peace became almost a

---

were hammered out. Even then it took almost three weeks just to organise the signing ceremony, which commenced at two o'clock in the afternoon of Saturday, October 24th, 1648.

23 Anabaptists (meaning "re-baptizers") represent a radical Protestant tradition tracing its history to the 16th century C.E. reformer Ulrich Zwingli. The Anabaptists were distinct because of their assertion of the necessity of adult baptism, rejecting the infant baptism practiced by the Roman Catholic Church. They believed that true baptism required a public confession of both sin and faith, which could only be accomplished as an adult exercise of free will. Another defining characteristic of Anabaptists is their belief in the separation of church and state, and the concept that the church represents the community of saved. Even though, the Anabaptist movement began in Zurich, Switzerland, it quickly spread to Moravia and throughout Germany. Many Anabaptists were persecuted in Europe, by both Roman Catholics and other Protestant groups, and most Anabaptist leaders were executed by the end of the 16th century C.E. However, in northern Germany and the Netherlands, pacifist Anabaptists rallied under the leadership of Menno Simons and survived the persecution. Menno's followers would eventually form the Mennonite tradition and become the only lasting Anabaptist tradition. The Mennonites continue to treasure the teachings of Menno, which include thoughts on pacifism, spirituality, and social ideas. Anabaptists, through the Mennonite tradition, are known for their separation from the world (including a refusal of military service), pacifism, radical discipleship, and simplicity of life.

24 Cf. Huizinga Johan, *Erasmus and the Age of Reformation* (New York: Harper, 1957), 110.

forgotten subject in the church. Meanwhile, the Church also felt that as they continued to exist in the world without peace between these two Churches, it becomes more difficult for them to see or realize the peace that was wished by their Lord Jesus Christ (John 16:33).[25] It was in 1557 that Western delegates visited the Eastern Church for peace initiatives. In 1573 another peacemaking and dialogue initiatives took place between these two warring churches. During these peacemaking and dialogue initiatives another severe conflict took place between the Roman Catholics and the Orthodox churches. In the process, there materializes three groups, i.e., Eastern Christianity (Orthodox), Western Christianity (Roman Catholic) and the Protestant Christianity (Western).[26]

Church History records that more than the political conflicts, the conflicts within the Christian church was more severe in nature. The then world was divided according to these conflicts. A notable person who was very involved in the peacemaking initiatives during this period was Cyril Loukaris (Orthodox).[27] He was a staunch advocate of peace among these warring groups.[28] He was executed by the Roman Catholics for taking peacemaking and dialogue initiative among the Christians in 1736. Other well-known peace-builders of those times were Marcius De Nointel, the Great Bishop and Peter the Great of Russia. They all took seriously the peacemaking and dialogue initiatives to bring peace among the Christians of different groups.[29] Despite the fact that the efforts of these leaders could not immediately resolve the conflicts among the Christians of different groups, they enabled

25 Cf. Euan Cameron, *The European Reformation* (Oxford and New York, 1991), 76.

26 Cf. Chadwick Owen, *The Popes and European Revolution* (Oxford: Oxford Press, 1981), 78.

27 Hugh McLeod, *Religion and the People of Western Europe, 1789-1989* (Oxford: Oxford Press, 1997), 78.

28 Cf. Michael Burleigh, *Earthly Powers: Religion and Politics in Europe from the Enlightenment to the Great War* (Oxford: Oxford Press, 2007), 109.

29 Cf. Constantine N. Callinicos, *The History of the Orthodox Church: A Brief Sketch of the One Holy Orthodox Catholic and Apostolic Church* (Los Angeles: Prothymos Press, 1957), 45.

the church to look further for the peaceful co-existence among themselves and the state.

Efforts of Peacemaking and Dialogue in the Church Continues till Today

It has become very hard to visualize peaceful Christians without conflicts amongst themselves. Without resolving misunderstanding and differences amongst themselves it was not, and is not, possible, to profess the true nature of the Church. Throughout the history of Christianity several peacemaking and dialogue initiatives have been taking place but without much success. Today, peacemaking and dialogue in and of the Church continues to struggle to have an effective impact. Churches are so much divided today due to geographical, political, cultural, language and doctrinal barriers or differences. All these factors continue to contribute difficulties to peaceful relations and coexistence in today's world.[30] Different churches have taken serious concern for peacemaking and dialogue initiatives in the churches and the World Council of Churches has created a unit that deals with the peace and justice in the world today.[31] At the international level, the WCC is playing an important role trying to create a peaceful living among the different denominations of Christianity as well as with people of other faiths.

Nationally, the churches are more aware today concerning peace and peacemaking and dialogue initiatives in the church as well as in the society. National Council of Churches in India (NCCI) has its Unit on peace and justice. NCCI is taking very active part in several conflict situations within the church and in the society. Almost all the member churches of NCCI have their own unit of peace and justice for carrying out peace mission/

30 Thomas F. Best, et.al., eds., *Growth in Agreement IV: International Dialogue Texts and Agreed Statements, 2005 – 2013, Volumes 1 and 2* (Geneva: WCC Publication, 2015), 56.

31 Olav Fykse Tveit, *The Truth We Owe Each Other Mutual Accountability in the Ecumenical Movement* (Geneva: WCC Publication, 2015), 25.

ministry in the church and society today.[32] This is how NCCI is taking peacemaking and dialogue toward not just the church and human society but also toward the well-being of the whole creation of God. Different churches in India have developed their own peacemaking efforts to counter various conflict situations. Church of South India (CSI), Church of North India (CNI), Council of Baptist Churches in North East India (CBCNEI), Presbyterian Church of India (PCI), Methodist Church in India (MCI), Orthodox Churches, Roman Catholic Churches, etc., have their own Peace and Justice Units that build peace among the different denominations and other living faiths in India as well as among varied conflict situations. Besides that, we also have local churches actively involved in peacemaking and dialogue missions and activities within their own given contexts, be it amidst inter-churches relations, communal or tribal conflicts, or amidst states, towns, militants and governments etc. The urgency of the task to overcome conflicts and violence is as apparent today as ever. The churches are challenged anew to respond to their calling to live as the peacemaking church of Jesus and to put his teachings into action. The Church and peacemaking network should be alive and growing. It should be sustained by its members' expectation that more and more Christians will commit themselves to Jesus' vision of the Church of Peace and journey together on a path of transformation.

Christian Peacemaking and Dialogue in India Today

India comprises of twenty nine states and six union territories and one capital union territory and considered as the most popular democratic country in the world today. India is considered to be having the distinction of having the largest population two of the three religions of the world today; Islam and Hinduism. India also has similar smaller religious minorities such as Christian, Buddhism and Sikhism. Religious turmoil has long been a fact

32 Grace Ji-Sun Kim, *Making Peace with the Earth: Action and Advocacy for Climate Justice Creating a Climate for Change* (Geneva: WCC Publication, 2016), 27.

life in India. Religious violence has claimed thousands of lives in India. Religious restrictions in India are found to be having one of the highest levels of social hostilities involving religion in the world today. In the present multi religious society in India the believers of different religions are called to live and grow in dialogue with persons of other religions. The importance of dialogues is such that peace and harmony need to experience within this multi religious society. Followers of different religions should open to the faith of other religions. There cannot be peace among the different religions without dialogue between them. Therefore, inter-religious dialogue is a challenge for the multi-religious society today.

The question of other faiths had been one of the main concerns of the postcolonial Christianity. This concern had led to the serious discussions on the concept of dialogue with other living faiths at important meeting and gathering of several Christian organizations today. India is a land of many religions, ideologies and cultures. Religion is a serious affair to every Indian. Indian spirituality is deeply rooted in Indian spiritual heritage. Religion and politics are inseparable in Indian tradition. Owing to this meddling of religion and politics, in these postcolonial days the religions have become a dividing and destructive force.[33] As a result, Christian faith has to be in constant dialogue with other living faiths.

In India, Churches, various associations and other groups and organizations have carried out the process of inter-faith dialogue with great importance. From about 1950, the CISRS, Bangalore, under the leadership of P.D. Devanandan and M.M. Thomas, pioneered in the studies about dialogue.[34] Vatican in 1964 opened a secretariat for Non-Christian Religions. In 1975 the WCC, Geneva, established section for dialogue with other living faiths. In 1975, the National Council of Churches in India started

33 Cf. Woba James, *Major Issues in the History of Christianity in India: A Post Colonial Reading* (Jorhat: TDCC Publications, 2013), 261.

34 Paul Tillich, *Christianity and the Religions of the World* (New York: Columbia University Press, 1963), 22.

a unit on Unity, Fellowship and Dialogue.[35] Since, then it had been playing a significant role in organizing several meetings and seminars on the inter-religious dialogue in connection with other interested bodies. We can briefly look into its several meetings.

i) A Live-in Dialogue with different religious groups was organized by the NCCI on July 9-10, 1991, at Kerala United Theological Seminary campus.[36]
ii) Hindu-Christian Dialogue was held in Varanasi on 9-12 February 1992. The theme of the Dialogue was "Our Heritage and Our Commitment to Harmony." About 65 Hindus and Christians for four days lived, discussed and prayed together, understanding the two religious traditions and common cultural heritage. The meeting resolved that new methods of inter-religious dialogue be initiated which will reach the rural masses, students in schools and colleges, and different audiences of children. It stated that inter-religious dialogue must address the problems of poverty and suffering. Religious traditions should be purged of elements of oppression and exploitation, particularly of women and weaker section of society.[37]
iii) Inter-religious Dialogue was conducted by the NCCI in June 1994 at Indian Social Institute, New Delhi. Leaders from different religions participated. The main concern was to bring in communal harmony and development through dialogue.[38]
iv) On 10-11 August 1994, NCCI and Henry Martyn Institute of Islamic Studies at Hyderabad organized an Inter-Faith Dialogue and Communalism. The main

35 Mathai Zachariah, *Beyond Ecumenism: A Journey in Light* (Thiruvalla: CSS, 2002), 80.

36 *Minutes of the Meetings of the NCCI, 1989-91* (Nagpur: NCCI, 1991), 100.

37 *Minutes of the Meetings of the NCCI, 1991-92* (Nagpur: NCCI, 1992), 96.

38 *Minutes of the Meetings of the NCCI, 1994* (Nagpur: NCCI, 1994), 82.

emphasis of the meeting was to bring together both secular and religious leaders of our community.[39]

v) The NCCI, WCC and Madurai Kamraj University organized a programme on Hindu-Christian Relations from 8-11 October 1995 at Madurai. About 40 participants including 5 women represented both the communities.[40] The aim of the meeting was to draw out a document on Hindu-Christian relations for the use of both the communities for practical living and theological reflection.[41]

vi) NCCI organized an Inter-Faith Dialogue meeting in Padhar, Orissa from 17-19 November 1995. The meeting resolved a practical step, i.e., inter-religious group to be organized at the district and village levels in Orissa.[42]

vii) On 13-15 December 1996 a Muslim-Christian Relations was organized by NCCI and Henry Martyn Institute of Islamic Studies along with UP Council of Churches at the Bishop Johnson College at Allahabad. The meeting concluded with an agreement that Muslims and Christians living in the pluralistic context of India have to work for deeper understanding and better collaboration between each other in order to uphold the values common to all religious people and build up a harmonious, peaceful and just society in our country.[43]

viii) In October 1997 at Varanasi, the NCCI and the UP Council of Churches organized a Hindu-Christian

---

39 *Minutes of the Meetings of the NCCI, 1995-96* (Nagpur: NCCI, 1996), 74.

40 Among the Hindus there were two swamijis - Swami Tattuvamayananda from Sri Ramakrishna Math, Thrissur and Swami Sadhashivananda, an organizer for Vishwa Hindu Parishad at Madurai. Among the Christians there were representatives from the NCCI, Churches, and the Roman Catholic Church, and Executive Secretary of Dialogue Unit of World Council of Churches.

41 *NCCI: Nagpur to Ranchi, 1996-1999* (Nagpur: NCCI, 1999), 2.

42 *NCCI: Nagpur to Ranchi, 1996-1999* (Nagpur: NCCI, 1999), 3.

43 *NCCI: Nagpur to Ranchi, 1996-1999* (Nagpur: NCCI, 1999), 11

Dialogue meeting. Delegates from various religious groups were present and the main emphasis of the dialogue was a cordial living among religious groups in India.[44]

ix) Inter-religious Consultation on National Issues was conducted by the NCCI on 19 August 2000. Religious leaders from different faiths attended the consultation. They resolved to organize more of such meeting in the near future.[45]

x) The first Inter-religious Dialogue in the North East India was organized by the NCCI and Thomas Jones School of Mission and Evangelism of Cherrapunji, from November 28 to December 1, 2000 at Cherrapunji, Meghalaya. 20 leaders of different faiths and about 40 theological students attended the meeting. The participants resolved to extend this inter-faith dialogue throughout the North East region.[46]

xi) The NCCI and YMCA New Delhi organized an Inter-faith Consultation on August 19, 2000 at the YMCA, New Delhi. More than 50 religious leaders and scholars belonging to Hinduism, Islam, Christianity, Buddhism, Jainism, Sikhism, Bahaism and Zoroastrianism participated in the Consultation. It resolved to establish Inter-religious Council of religious leaders of India and an Inter-religious Pilgrimage to be conducted to Mathura so as to soothe the tension and communal violence there.[47]

xii) Inter-Faith Dialogue for Better living was organized by NCCI and Christian Forum on 7 May 2001 at Pune.

---

44 *NCCI: Nagpur to Ranchi, 1996-1999* (Nagpur: NCCI, 1999), 17.

45 *NCCI: Meetings of the Executive Committee and General Body, 3-4 August, 2001*, 15.

46 *NCCI: Meetings of the Executive Committee and General Body, 3-4 August, 2001*, 17.

47 *NCCI: Meetings of the Executive Committee and General Body, 3-4 August, 2001*, 32.

People from various walks of life such as priests, theologians and leaders of different faiths participated and pledged to see that their regions are kept violent-free and to live with respect and understanding.[48]

xiii) On September 11 2001, the NCCI and the Rashtriya Swayamsevak Sangh (RSS) conducted an Inter-Faith Dialogue in Nagpur. The meeting resolved to continue dialogue between them with mutual respect and understanding for each other's traditions and beliefs.[49]

xiv) The Madurai Kamaraj University with NCCI conducted a Seminar on Inter-Faith Dialogue on 31 May 2002 at Madurai. The participants from different faiths prayed for the peace and communal harmony in the country.[50]

The dialogue movement shows that people of diverse faiths while disagreeing in beliefs, can agree on the importance of peace and justice, of social action to relieve suffering and on efforts to save the planet. Inter-faith dialogue is particularly essential in a religiously plural context such as India where communal conflict is currently dividing the country.[51] The reality of religious pluralism as well as the validity of different beliefs and way of life needs to be accepted, and dialogue can help create this understanding, for dialogue in its essence is the acceptance and respect of one another irrespective of caste, creed, colour, race or culture.

Therefore in this context, the national integration, nation's unity and sovereignty and people's harmonious existence together solely depend on meaningful and sincere inter-religious dialogue. In India, a pluralistic context, people of different faiths and no faiths have to work together, pool together in the building of our harmonious nation. The Churches should realize that dialogue with

48 *NCCI: Meetings of the Executive Committee and General Body, 3-4 August, 2001*, 18.

49 *The NCCI Meeting of the Executive Committee and General Body, 6-7 August, 2002*, 10.

50 *The NCCI Meeting of the Executive Committee and General Body, 6-7 August, 2002*, 12.

51 Woba James, *Major Issues*… 264.

other religions and ideologies are inevitable as far as the Christian mission is concerned, and the Church has to make all efforts to enlarge its scope. The Church must stand in solidarity with the rest of the total community in its struggle for greater human dignity and fuller human existence. As shown, dialogue with other living faiths has been an effective tool for ecumenical advance between diverse faiths. They have been able to put centuries old conflicts to some extent into new life and thus have enabled different religions in varying degrees to move beyond these controversies. The dialogue of the future will continue to offer new hopes, for the different peoples and religions of the world.

Conclusion

Reflecting upon the biblical truth – the source and basis of our Christian faith and life, God's very act of creation tells us that the God who we believe in is the God of life, of peace, of order and of relationships. Peace (*Shalom*) is at the heart of God's intention for creation. The Church as the follower of Christ is called to practice peacemaking and dialogue today. The history of the Christian church since its inception had to grapple with the variegated forms of conflicts and tensions – at the political-religious and internal-external level. The greatest of all challenges for the church down through the centuries, was to wrestle with the reality of tensions, conflicts and differences that threatened the sanctity, commitment and peace of the church and society. In the midst of such situations and times we also see God's healing intentions and peace for the church and the people. Peacemaking and dialogue initiatives were time and again undertaken by the churches and their leaderships. They put all their efforts to bring together the church and the state, and between the two warring groups of Christianity - that of Eastern and Western Christianity. With the great schism that took place in 1054 the conflict situation worsened. Yet there were always peace-loving groups that continued to strive for peace even at the risk of their own lives. Till today we continue to witness the Christians taking initiatives for peacemaking and dialogue at different levels of conflict situations and thus, whether we agree or not, the fact remains that Christians' role in peacemaking and dialogue cannot be ignored. At the same time, Christians should also be wisely self-critical of the elements of dissensions, rivalries and violence that are often found embedded deep within our own fold, that render us 'disabled' in carrying out peacemaking and dialogue not just within ourselves but also toward the world outside – God's wider household – people of other living faiths and the world of creation.

3

Interfaith Relations in a Pluralistic Society A Theological Reconsideration

***Shanbha Hayong*[1]**

Introduction

The word 'pluralism' originates from the Latin word *Pluralis* meaning many or more in numbers. Etymologically, it may be referred as the "quality or state of being plural." Oxford Dictionary defines it as "the existence or toleration in society of a number of groups that belong to different races or have different political or religious belief."[2] It signifies how people from different groups and backgrounds living together share their life experiences in one and a composite community. Whether one likes it or not, he/she is destined to live together. It is a fact of human life. It is God's will that people should live and share life together. Each and every individual is born and brought up in different and particular ethnic group, bound to speak different languages, belong to different cultures, follow different religions but in spite of all differences they are intended to live, share and journeying life together.

---

1 Rev. Dr. Shanbha Hayong is an Associate Professor, Department of Theology and Ethics at John Roberts Theological Seminary, Mawklot, Shillong.

2 Catherine Soanes, *Compact Oxford Dictionary Thesaurus & Word Power Guide* (Oxford: Oxford University Press, 2001), 679.

Pluralistic Nature of the Indian Society

Indian society is a pluralistic society. There is adequate space for different races, ethnic groups, languages, castes, tribes, religious ideologies, faith, cultures, etc. Indian society could accommodate diverse kinds of communities who profess different faith, practice different religions, speak different languages but live together in a large community maintaining the spirit of harmony and co-existence even though tension and conflict taking place time and again.[3] This pluralistic nature of the country offer immense opportunities and privileges to different communities as they venture together towards building up a better future. In turn, it has tremendously contributed to the richness and prosperity of the Indian society. But even though pluralism has its own positive contribution to the society, in due course in such a multi-cultural and multi-religious context peaceful co-existence and communal harmony has been threaten from time to time. Samartha rightly pointed out when he states that though the pluralistic situation has its own beauty and gift to the society it has always created chaos as evident in the history of the Indian people.[4]

Pluralism: A Blessing

Diversity of human communities is created and sustained by God. Pluralism is part of God design and purpose. It is the gift of God to humanity. In the Indian context for quite a long time, Indian people learnt to live together and uphold the spirit of unity in diversity. Indian people were regarded as tolerant and big hearted having the ability to accommodate multiplicity of cultures, races, ethnic groups and religious practices. This rich diversity and plurality of peoples groups and cultures can be considered as the gift of God to Indian people. They are like different types of flowers blooming

3 S.J. Samartha, "Inter-religious Relationship in a Secular State," in *Inter-Faith Dialogue and World Community,* edited by Ch. Sreenivasa Rao (Madras: CLS 1991), 56-57.

4 S.J. Samartha, "Inter Religious Relationship in the Secular State," in *The Multi Faith Context of India: Resources and Challenges for Christians,* edited by Israel Selvarayagan (Bangalore: BTTBPSA, 1994), 1.

with varieties of colors and beautiful designs in the garden of India. Consequently, Indian people as they live together confronting and encountering each other in their daily life experiences come to realize that their differences are enriching.[5] Pluralistic context like India offer an opportunity to its people to learn from each other through mutual sharing of their resources and experiences. This phenomenon definitely calls the attention of the right thinking people about the inescapable fact of interdependence and interrelationship of people and communities and the bonding solidarity that binds and unites humankind. Pluralism should be viewed not as something that hinder or obstruct peaceful co-existence and communal harmony but as a situation that provide opportunities for a creative and viable growth and development of a better community.

The Other Side of Pluralism

Though the bright side of pluralism is much convincing and offers better scope for peaceful co-existence, on the other hand it has its own problem of varied forms. Today one could testifies to the emergence of different varieties of tensions and conflicts in many pluralistic society which has threaten the very fabric of harmonious living and peaceful co-existence among diverse communities that have been living together for many centuries. Amalados pointed out two significant problems of pluralism among many.[6] The first problem occurs when one group tries to dominate the others even to the extent of eliminating their identity or reduce them to subjection. The outcome of such act is the outburst of serious conflict for the subaltern group would fight against all sort of domination and suppression for protecting their identity. The second problem is that, when there is an attempt to develop some sorts of unity out of the diverse forms of cultures and traditions by suppressing differences and imposing one culture, the dominant culture as a replacement. The weaker groups incapable to withstand such act accept it in their own way without

5 Michael Amalados S.J., *Making Harmony*, (Delhi: IDCR& ISPCK, 2003), 1.

6 Amalados, *Making Harmony,* 8.

really detaching from their respective original culture. This points to the fact that pluralism despite of all its positive contribution to the good and better welfare of humanity is being exploited and manipulated by the dominant group who exerts its power and authority over the vulnerable weaker sections of the society for their selfish gains. Though one cannot ignore the problems caused by other components of pluralism, here, the main concentration will be on the challenges posed by religious pluralism especially in a pluralistic society like India.

Religious Pluralism: A Reality in many Societies

Religious pluralism refers to the fact that different religions with different backgrounds and traditions exist together in specific place or region. T. Swami Raju argues that religious pluralism means, "Different religions exist as diverse means of knowing and experiencing God or the ultimate one reality in a culturally, historically and linguistically familiar way."[7] Different religious traditions imply diverse response to the mystery of God the ultimate reality in a way that is best suited to the concern community. At present, the current understanding of religious pluralism may be referred to the context where different faith communities exist side by side as they journey together in their attempt to search for the Ultimate Truth. In such a multi-religious situation living contact and sharing religious experience among diverse faith communities is not an option but a reality. Religious pluralism reflects the richness of God's creation. Such a situation is in no way to be exploited or manipulated for selfish gain, rather need to be acknowledged and accepted as divine gifts to humanity.

Religious pluralism has become a reality not only in the context of India or in Asia but it is also a reality in many western countries. One could witness many Hindu temples and Muslim mosque in different cities of western countries which testifies that religious pluralism is no more confined or limited to one geographical area or territory but its presence is recognized in

7 T. Swami Raju, *Christian Responses to Plurality of Religion* (Bangalore: BTESSC/SATHRI, 2006), 36.

many world societies.[8] In the present day era of globalization with the entire world is reduced to a global village migration and movement of population from one place to another or one territory to another in search for employment or better living has become a continuous process. M.M. Thomas clearly makes a point in his statements when he says:

> The migration of ethnic and religious groups across national and continental boundaries enhances the pluralistic character of all societies so that pluralism today is not merely a global phenomenon; it has also become local and national.[9]

Simultaneously, political alliance and trade relations between countries, different varieties of exchange programs, influence of media and the like offer extensive exposure for many people to different cultures and religions of the world. This trend not only give way for many societies to accommodate diverse groups of population but it has change many traditional societies into religiously pluralistic society. For a pluralistic society like India where religious diversity for many centuries is a reality this trend is nothing new, but for other societies in western countries, engaging and living together alongside with people of other faith is a new challenge. As mentioned above, pluralism or to be specific religious pluralism provides ample opportunities for mutual enrichment and harmonious living through sharing of resources and learning from each other faith traditions. Despite several advantages that religious pluralism offers to the society, living together alongside neighbors of other faith, with different belief, perception and understanding of reality, has rather bring many unpleasant stories that could hamper and shatter the very foundation of peaceful co-existence and harmonious living as testifies in the history of India.

---

8 R.E. Hedlund, "Religious Pluralism: Fact and Issue. An Introductory Essay," in *Many Other Ways? Question of Religious Pluralism*, edited by M. Bage, et al., (Delhi: ISPCK, 1992), 13.

9 M.M. Thomas, *Risking Christ for Christ's Sake: Towards an Ecumenical Theology of Pluralism* (Geneva: WCC Publications, 1987), 2.

Politicization of Religion

Coming to the Indian context, the founders of modern India accepted and adopted a secular nationalism as the foundation of Indian constitutional democracy. Each and every individual has the freedom to believe, to choose or adopt any religious traditions and no organizations or groups has the right to impinge or interrupt anyone with regards to his or her faith. Article 25 of the Indian constitution guarantee freedom to all people to profess and propagate their belief in any religious traditions. But the BJP and its ally emphasize on communal identity with a dream of creating a Hindu Rashtra or Hindu Nation.[10] They have a belief that to be an Indian is to be a Hindu. Hence, they tend to think that whatever is Hindu is absolute therefore need to be accepted by every person identifies himself and herself as Indian.[11] They even go to the extent claiming that all primal faith are part and parcel of Hindu tradition, therefore, they make an attempt to emphasize that religious and cultural values of the tribal and indigenous people are nothing but essential components of a broader Hindu traditions. Ninan Koshy argues that "there is tendency to interpret religious values and even religious practices in terms of the majority religion's conception."[12] For instance, today one could observe a close connection between the RSS and the traditional Khasi religion in Meghalaya through different collaboration programs in different parts of the land.[13] This new development is carried on with the understanding that all primal faith within the country existing since time immemorial is very much part of the Hindu religious tradition.

---

10 MG Devasahayam, "Peace and Political Predicament," in *Political Governance in a Multi-Religious World*, edited by Moses P. Monohar (Delhi: ICSA/ISPCK, 2004), 75.

11 Ninan Koshy, "The Christian Community in a Secular State," in *Christian Witness in Society*, edited by K.C. Abraham (Bangalore: Board of Theological Education-Senate of Serampore College, 1998), 85.

12 Koshy, *The Christian Community in a Secular State*, 85.

13 At present the RSS has provide financial assistance and sponsored many tribal student especially the poor section free of cost to study in different parts of India.

The Hindutva ideology of one nation, one culture and one religion not only create tension among different communities but threaten the peaceful atmosphere of Indian society. Minorities like Muslims and Christians are already out of the picture. In recent years, blatant attack against the Dalits in many places at different times, the Sikh riots in 1984,[14] demolition of Babri Masjid in 1992,[15] the Gujarat episode in 2002[16] and its aftermath where thousands of life lost and property destroyed without any mercy, are some but glaring example that shake the very foundation of a secular India.[17] In recent years the main target was directed against Christians and Christian institutions. Frequent attack on different Churches, Bibles burned, missionary and Church workers are violently persecuted and harassed and so on.[18] Politicization of religion by the BJP and its ally raised number of questions with regard to the nature and relevancy of the secular state in a pluralistic country like India. Is the majority religious community has the sole right to impose their religious values on the minorities? What is the

14 The anti-Sikh riot in 1984 is referred to the anti-Sikh pogrom and violent activities directed towards the Sikh community in response to the assassination of Mrs. Indira Gandhi by her Sikh bodyguards that led to the massacre of thousands of Sikh people across India. https://www.quora.com/what-happenedin-1984-anti-Sikh-riots (Access on 20 March 2017).

15 Demolition of Babri Masjid or the Ayodya incidents is taken place on the 6th December 1992 and its aftermath when the VHP and its associates where around 1,50,000 *karsevaks* attacked and demolished the Babri Masjid that resulted to the killing of thousands of people especially the Muslims in many Indian cities. https://en.wikipedia.org/wiki/Ayodhya_dispute (Access on 20 March 2017).

16 Godhra episode occurred on the 27th February 2002 when the Sabarmati Express was burned in Godhra in which 59 Hindu pilgrims who were returning from Ayodhya after a religious ceremony at the disputed Babri Mosque were killed in the burning of the above train. This resulted to the counter clash between Muslims and Hindus that led to the killing of thousands of Muslims. https://www.soundvision.com/article/what-happened-in-godhra-gujurat (Access on 20th March 2017).

17 Ipe Joseph, "Towards a Spirituality of Pilgrimage: Interfaith Co-operation in South Asia," in *Building Spirituality and the Culture of Peace*, edited by P.G. Widyatmatja (Hongkong: URM/CCA, 2004), 138.

18 Ram Puniyani, *Facism of Sangh Parivar* (Delhi: Media House, 2002), 7.

place and role of minorities in the present day Indian democracy? Do they have no right to contribute to towards nation building? Their voices are being ignored and sidelined. Several attempts to suppress and silence their voices and frequent effort to eradicate their space in the mainstream of the society today tend to become an issue of great concern. It has raised certain doubt not only about the secular nature of the country and on many occasions even their presence seems to be unwanted to those groups striving towards making India Hindu nation. Koshy rightly argues when he states:

> The politics of the BJP has raised fundamental questions about the nature of Indian nationalism, the meaning of secularism and the role of the minorities. It has a pragmatic mythology that cannot only alter the course of the mainstream politics but also change the character of the nation. Any attempt to underestimate the nature of the threat will only promote the divisive forces.[19]

At the time of partition Indian leaders opt for a secular state justifying their choice that only a "secular political framework can provide neutral space for people of different religious persuasions and ideological convictions to make their contribution to the value bases of the nation."[20]Any attempt to alter the secular nature of the country has blurred and distorted the vision of the freedom fighters and their attempt to make India home for all sections of population irrespective of the caste, class, races, ethnic and religious background, and so on. If that is the case the very basis and foundation in which the nation is establish and strengthen as a secular and democratic country is being shaken. Religious conflicts frequently emerged during the last few decades bear witness that the secular state has failed to provide genuine space for different religious communities. The end result is that such tensions and conflicts left deep impact on different sections of population especially the minorities. Minorities especially the religious minorities are struggling for a genuine space within the mainstream of the societies making all efforts proclaiming that

19 Koshy, *The Christian Community in a Secular State*, 86.

20 Samartha, *Inter-religious Relationship in the Secular State*, 59.

they have something good to contribute towards nation building. Though many a times their voices are being sideline it has nevertheless redirect the attention of the nation towards the very basis and foundation in which the country is established. Such a situation demands proper understanding of religion and its role in a pluralistic country like India.

Study of Religion

Politicization of religion by the vested interest groups making it an instrument for political gain and exert pressure by the dominant community over the minorities in their attempt towards building up one nation, one culture and one religion entails genuine and comprehensive understanding of the role of religion in the society especially a pluralistic society like India. Such a venture demands for a better analytical study of religion not in isolation but a comparative study of different religions and their place and role both in the nation and the history of human community as well. It is natural but true when one attempts to understand religion apart from his or her own tradition it is often biased leading to the misrepresentation of other religious faith. There is a tendency to claim and asserts that one's own religion is better than the other. But a better understanding of religion will be materialized only when one make efforts for a comparative understanding of religion or a relational conception of religion. Each and every religion is understood and considered as a living faith that provide certain directions and guiding principles to its adherent in their search for the ultimate truth. Addressing the importance of a comparative study of religion Santosh Sen Gupta plainly maintains when he says "What is necessary is that it (religion) should be studied as a living faith of the practicing believers." He further elaborates this as he asserts "the study of religion as living faiths provides an insight into the essential connectedness or the unity of the different religions."[21]The emergence of different religious traditions

21 Santosh Sen Gupta, "On the Understanding of Other Religions," in *Interfaith Dialogue and World Community*, edited by Ch. Sreenivasa Rao (Madras: The Christian Literature Society, 1991), 22.

testifies the reality of different responses to the mystery of the divine. Here, it is significant to say that many religions emerged in a religiously plural environment and in the process shaped its feature in reaction to that pluralism.[22] If that is the case any attempt to have a proper understanding of religion is to study one religion in relation to another. Gupta maintains that "each religion is to be viewed as a human phenomenon as relative to a particular situational complex of the cultural life of the people. Now to study one situational complex in isolation from another is to commit the error of abstraction."[23]

It may be noted that different religion evolved after a long search for the ultimate truth by a particular community in a specific location in accordance with the situation best suited to them. As it is a response to one ultimate truth the essential values of each religion in the first place are complementary rather than contradictory. The basic essences and core values of each religion contains the message of love, peace, justice and the like. In due course throughout the entire history of faith communities many among the religious communities tend to depart from the basic important teaching of their respective religion. The emergence of different vested interest within a particular religion began to exploit the loopholes for their selfish interest. In the name of religion they go to a certain extent to exert their dominance over the other especially the weaker section of humanity. This is best explain in the following statement

> Although, the core values of all religions are complementary rather than contradictory, what is happening is that religions contradict the core values that correspond to them. The shell is idolized, and the life-nourished kernel is discarded. The resultant spiritual bankruptcy is exploited by vested interests.

22 Harold Coward, *Pluralism: Challenge to World Religions* (Delhi: Sri Satguru Publications, 1985), 94.

23 Gupta, *On the Understanding of Other Religion*, 23.

> Religion, which is meant to be a school of love, peace and justice, becomes a call to hatred, oppression and cruelty.[24]

This entails, to help solve the myriad problems evolved in interfaith relationship, that all religions necessarily need to revisit ad reconsider their core values that are life affirming and liberating so that each and every religion could contribute towards a healthy relationship among adherents of all faith communities especially as they are living together in a pluralistic society. If different religious traditions come together and rediscovered and reinterpret the essential values of their respective religion it will of course become immense contribution towards peaceful co-existence and harmonious living in the process of building up a better society.

Reaffirming the Theology of Interfaith Relations

In the last few decades India witnessed diverse kind of religious intolerance and religious conflicts erupted among different faith communities that has threaten the very fabric of peaceful co-existence and harmonious living. In turn, such a situation has ruins and hampers interfaith relations that may take a long time to heal and return back to normal. The long term and healthy interfaith relationship that has been build up for many centuries is randomly destroyed within a moment of interfaith clashes and conflicts. The increasing religious violence and violence related acts has threatened the peace and security of the country and dismantle the secular nature of India. Confronting with such a dishearten situation people turned towards religion for solution of the problems. However, being part of the problem it is not an easy task for different religions to provide genuine answers to the peoples' query. What can religion offer in the midst of religious tensions and conflicts? Whatever the case may be, people still believed that religion has something to offer. It is therefore, a clarion call to different religious traditions for collective effort and joint endeavor in the process of eradicating religious conflicts

24 Carlos Evaristo Da Gama, *The Christian Struggle for a New Society* (Mumbai: The Bombay Saint Paul Society, 2002), 154.

that has damaged the peaceful atmosphere within the country. This demand for the responsibility of not only one particular religious tradition but people of all faith communities need to come together striving towards achieving peace and harmony. M. Deenabandhu argues "peace is not an ideal state that can be search for, or journey towards but to be struggled for."[25]

From Co-existence to Co-operation

Living in a pluralistic society each faith community is expected to maintain the atmosphere of peaceful co-existence. Indian people is well known as tolerant people that could maintain the spirit of unity in diversity despite many forces that attempt to thwart the bond that bind together Indian people for many centuries back. However, to sustain the spirit of oneness among the people in a multi faith context like India, faith communities have to move forward from mere co-existence to co-operation in building up interfaith relations. While mere co-existence may be understood as the ability to keep and maintain peace, co-operation calls for action. It necessitates active participation and collective effort engaging different faith communities to work for common issues affecting not only human society but the entire creation of God. It is a call to all faith communities to freely share and contribute their resources without any reservation as they wrestle together to solve different problems affecting the growth and well-being of the country's population as well as the surrounding environment. All faith communities are expected to commit themselves and dedicate their services as they venture together for the better welfare of humanity and the surrounding environment at large. For, without going beyond mere tolerance and peaceful co-existence and offering sincere collaboration in common tasks, the danger of falling into fundamentalist and fanatical postures and exacerbating inter-religious conflicts will not wither away.[26]

---

25 M. Deenabandhu, "Challenge for Peace in the New Millenium: A Fresh Look at the Concerns of the India Peace Centre," in *NCCR*, Vol. CXXI/5 (June 2001), 362.

26 Da Gama, *The Christian Struggle for a New Society,* 158.

Journeying Together as Community of Faith

In a pluralistic society like India, no religion could isolate itself from the other. Each religion as a living faith has in one way or the other developed some kinds of relationship with the other on many occasions and in different capacities. This entails that each religion need to be recognized, accepted and respected in the process of moving forward towards a better future. As they journey together in search of the Ultimate Truth, identity of each religion need to be protected and not to be distorted. Speaking on this issue from the perspective of Christianity Da Gama maintains that the Church is to be perceived as "a community in pilgrimage with people of other faiths towards the Kingdom that is to come." He further states that "interreligious dialogue is an ongoing process of common search for mutual understanding and trust, leading us and our fellow pilgrimage towards a deeper understanding of truth-truth about God and the human person."[27] In the process of walking alongside other faith communities the need to recognize each religion not as enemy but as partner or ally as they work together against the forces of evil that have distorted the notion of peace and harmonious living in a pluralistic society like India. Here, it requires that each faith community has to engage actively as powerful agent of social transformation working with full commitment towards building up a community of peace and justice. A multi-religious society where each religion has a space and all faith are valued and respected is an ideal community for the present day multi-religious world. In such a context each religion will live to its identity while at the same time have the opportunity to share their spiritual and ethical values that will guide human person towards a better future. Religion is to be understood not in comparison against the other but in relation to other. It is a context that provides room to diverse faith communities to flourish and prosper without encroaching each other space. Da Gama obviously terms this as "new model of democratic society." He further states "This new order will be respectful of diversity and particularity. It will have to move through consensus rather than

27 Da Gama, *The Christian Struggle for a New Society,* 156.

through the domination of a majority."[28]A multi religious society that respect and recognize the value of each faith community not only capable to maintain the spirit of unity in diversity but also experience the blessing of religious pluralism that could enrich life in many respect.

Revisiting our Faith Tradition

In order to build up interfaith relations in a pluralistic society one need to re-visit his or her own faith tradition with the aim of correcting certain drawbacks present in the tradition. It may be noted that all religions even though contain many good characteristics, in some way or the other possess some drawbacks that need serious attention and reconsideration. Many among us Christian are born and brought up in the atmosphere that make us believed and understand that Christianity is the only true religion and all other religions are false and doom to perish. Such conception makes one to believe Christian Church is the only religion that God has chosen to experience the mystery of the divine. It is through the Church that God manifests and revealed him/herself and other religions if they aspire to experience the mystery of the divine they have but to turn to Christianity the only religion that could embody the truth of the divine. It seems to reflect an attitude that considers "other religions as merely natural and human efforts to reach God, whereas Christianity represents God supernatural answer to human desire."[29] Exclusive claim of such nature affects the relationship between different faith communities which creates hurdles to peaceful coexistence while at the same time hamper the possibilities to work together for common good. Samartha asserts that such claim raised basic theological question about God's relationship with people of other faith. He further

28 Da Gama, *The Christian Struggle for a New Society,* 158.

29 Michael Amaladoss, *Walking Together: The Practice of Inter-religious Dialogue* (Anand: Gujarat Sahitya Prakash, 1992), 169.

suggests that "Christian need to move from normative exclusivism towards relational distinctiveness of Christ."[30]

In the process of searching the valid and genuine understanding of the reality of the divine it is well fitted to say that no religious tradition could claim absolute knowledge with regards to the reality about God. History tells us that when any religion make exclusive and absolute claims of truth "aggressive militancy and divisive proselytism follow, and in their wake bitter religious divisions."[31] This needs to be seriously reconsidered taking into account the element of divine truth presence in other faith traditions and experiences by their adherents. In the present contemporary theological debate where each religion deserve respect and recognition the exclusive terms often used by Christians like 'crusades,' 'Onward Christian soldiers,' and 'Stand up for Jesus…ye soldiers of the cross," need to be seriously considered whether are still relevant in the present day context of religious pluralism. Such negative attitude towards other faiths traditions instead of building up the spirit of unity in diversity has rather creating more distance between faith communities. Referring to the exclusive claim about the truth by the Church, Jacob Kavunkul as cited by R.E. Hedlund argues that "the Church has no monopoly on spiritual treasures."[32] Plurality in general and religious pluralism in particular is design by God since the beginning, hence; need to be accepted as divine gift to humanity. All religions are expected to accept pluralism as God given and natural. Since the time of creation, God has actively reached out to all people and religions through his word and the spirit.[33] It is not wrong to say that glimpse of the divine or divine spark is present in different religions of the world. In the context of interfaith relations each religion need to be understood not against the other

30 Stanley J. Samartha, "The Cross and the Rainbow: Christ in a Multi-Religious Culture," in *Christian Faith and Multiform Culture in India*, edited by Somen Das (Bangalore: United Theological College, 1987), 16.

31 Da Gama, *The Christian Struggle for a New Society*, 156.

32 Hedlund, Religious Pluralism: Fact and Issue. An Introductory Essay, 14.

33 Da Gama, *The Christian Struggle for a New Society*, 156.

but in relation to other. Any religion that decline to accept the reality of a pluralistic society has already isolated itself from others.[34] But there is a danger here if one compares his or her religion with the intention to project the best of his or her religion with the drawbacks of the other. This proves to be true in the words of Ajith Fernando when he says that "there are those who try the present a case for Christianity by appealing to the failure of non-Christians."[35] This trend is not healthy for it creates fracture to the fragile situation that would lead to bitter experience among different religious faith communities. In the context of religious pluralism understanding the place of religion and its role to both humanity and society need to be taken into account. In recent past there emerged an interest from the side of Christianity to realize the real values of other faith traditions and theology is expected to reconsider seriously the relationship of Christianity towards other faith. This demand for a serious reconsideration by different faith traditions or else exclusive claim of one religion will continue to obstruct peaceful co-existence and "the very principle which should be a source of peace for the world will continue to be a source of conflict."[36]

Interfaith Dialogue

Interfaith dialogue has become an important component that could build up interfaith relations especially in the midst of tensions and conflicts frequently surface among many religious communities. Most often dialogue is taking place at two levels-formal and informal level.[37] At the formal level it refers to the

---

34 Ibrahim Abdullah, "Religion as Source and Remedy of Conflict," in *World Religions in Dialogue: Co-operating to Transform Society*, edited by Henry.O. Thomson (Delhi: ISPCK, 1993), 16.

35 Ajith Fernando, *Relating to People of Other Faiths* (Mumbai: GLS Publishing, 1989), 75.

36 Fr. Bede Griffiths, "Religious Truth and Relationship between Religions," in *Inter-Faith Dialogue and World Community*, edited by Ch. Sreenivasa Rao (Madras: Christian Literature Society, 1991), 3.

37 Felix Wilfred, "Inter-religious Dialogue as a Political Question," in *Christian Witness in Society*, edited by K.C. Abraham (Bangalore:

dialogue that has been formally arranged at different levels where discussions, deliberations and sharing of resources by different faith communities based on certain issues related with doctrines, worldviews, ideals and other common issues affecting human person and the society. At the informal level it is referred to the dialogue of life in which one person come into contact with another in their daily life struggles and living experiences within a community.

Interfaith dialogue means to talk to each other. It means to know each other in a better way. It is a fact that communal disharmony occurs due to misunderstanding between religious communities. Dialogue offers an opportunity to know better about their belief, worldviews, concern, hope and the like which in turn help both parties having a common desire for peace and harmony. It is encouraging that series of dialogue taking place among different world religions. The development of science and technology, the role of media and so on that has shrunk the world into a global village provide good arena for better climate of dialogue. In the contemporary climate of dialogue partner become conscious that other religions apart from the one they profess have their respective space and need to be recognized and respected. They also have good and important teachings that could help benefitted not only their adherents but the entire humanity. There are many positive elements presence in other faiths apart from their respective faith traditions that could contribute profoundly towards the better welfare of humanity. Nevertheless, despite such realization and the better ambiance for better co-operation through dialogue "the way of faith is not yet free from an attitude of separateness or exclusiveness and this has given rise to one major problem of understanding of other religion."[38] The followers of each and every religion still believed that their respective faith tradition is better than the other in many aspects. The positive elements possess by the other faith traditions have lesser value in comparison to their religious values in different capacities. Hence,

BTESSC, 1998), 187.

38 Gupta, *On the Understanding of Others Religions*, 21.

unless each religion gets rid of the claims that they are better than the other, successful and meaningful outcome of dialogue seems to be a distant reality.

Secondly, most of the interfaith dialogue in India today are not only taking initiative by Christians but also organized by Christians. As such, the entire program and deliberation turn out to be an all Christian affairs with limited impact occurs on the dialogue partner that belong from other faith. The outcome of many dialogue programs turn out to be far from the expectation and could not satisfied either of the dialogue parties. This need to be taken into account and considered seriously by those taken initiative for dialogue, otherwise many of the arranged programs will not arrive at the anticipated goal. Paulos Mar Gregarious rightly mentions when he argues that "Hindu believe not without justification that dialogue is a new form of western mission." It rather indicates that partner of dialogue from other faith traditions view dialogue with suspicious that such programs arrange to promote and project Christian faith. He further states that "Christian often forms majority of participants, and dominate and control dialogue, sometimes imposing their categories and often elements of their culture on the participants."[39] Dialogue is to be understood as being open to other faith traditions with the aim to glimpse how God is at work with them while at the same time makes all effort to realized how God's activity in them is related with what God has done among the Christian faith.

Thirdly, another important concern with regards to interfaith dialogue is that dialogue today is most often understood as having seminar, debate, symposium, consultation, conference, etc., on certain issues related with interfaith relation. But there is a wide gap between such academic and intellectual top level meeting and the masses at the grass root level. It is important to note that these formal well arranged gatherings though they have many positive outcome especially for the dialogue party it has nevertheless nothing much to do with the suffering of the marginalized poor.

39 Paulos Mar Gregorios, *Religion and Dialogue* (Kottayam: Margregorios Foundation, 2000), 189-190.

The end result is that while the debate and consultation continues millions of the impoverished poor go hungry with little hope of having a better future.[40] A meaningful and successful dialogue could happen only when it take into consideration the plight and suffering of the marginalized poor. This necessitates the urgent call to all faith communities to freely share their resources and values without any reservation together with the commitment to work together for the common welfare of humanity. It rather pose a challenge to all the members involved to see that all activities "ought to be directed towards collaborative action to build up a more just and humane society."[41] Interfaith dialogue does not mean mere encounter of two religious faiths. At the same time, it does not means mere encounter of religious commitment and belief. It is more than the meeting of faith. It is sharing. Hence, it has to take the life experience of the masses as the starting point of discussion. That is, dialogue need to be liberative and life affirming.

Fourthly, another concern with regards to interfaith dialogue is that, it does not take into consideration the indigenous people's spirituality as the point of departure in their theological debates. Indigenous people's spirituality and religious values have many things to offer towards the betterment of humanity. But their resources and life affirming cultural elements are being sidelines in the present contemporary theological dialogue. There is a feeling that unless indigenous people's resources are taken seriously as the important component of interfaith dialogue, indigenous people together with their religious and cultural values will be disregarded and ignored as something inferior devoid of anything good. A. Wati Longchar rightly argues when he says "for the indigenous people the basis for dialogue are not just common

40 Israel Sylvanayagam, *A Dialogue on Dialogue: Reflections on Interfaith Encounters* (Madras: The Christian Literature Society, 1995), 2.

41 Da Gama, *The Christian Struggle for a New Society,* 157.

humanization, spiritual enrichment, and option for the poor but an option for the integrity of creation."[42]

Conclusion

In the midst of religious tensions and conflicts emerged in the present day contemporary society interfaith relation is not only necessary but mandatory. In a pluralistic society like India to have a peaceful co-existence and harmonious living co-operation among different faith is necessary. But this could be done only if all faith communities are open to each other sharing their resources and religious values as they work together in the process of nation building. It implies that all faith communities need to work together as agent of transformation making the society a better place that give space to all section of population.

42 A. Wati Longchar, "Inter-Religious Theological Methodology from the Location of Indigenous People in Asia," in *Inter-Cultural Asian Theological Methodologies: An Exploration*, edited by Samson Prabhakar (Bangalore: South Asia Theological Research Institute, 2002), 73.

4

Cosmic Interdependence Primal Indigenous/Tribal Perspective for Inter-Religious Harmony

Eyingbeni Hümtsoe-Nienu[1]

Introduction

The reality of religious plurality in India is as ancient as the religions themselves, with most being born in India like Hinduism and its offshoots – Buddhism, Sikhism and Jainism or introduced to India in the early years of its birth like Christianity and Islam. The other category of religion that mostly goes unattended is the primal/ indigenous tribal religion. Although, tribals form a total of 8.6% (2011) of India's 1.2b population, there are variation in culture and history among them, mostly determined by geographical region. Hence, the tribal communities of the Northeast (NE) are the focus of this paper, owing to obvious commonality shared among them than with any other tribal groups in India. The NE including Sikkim has a population of 40m (2011), a mere 3.1% of Indian population. However, tribal concentration in the region is significant for possibly forming the largest tribal group in India. The state-wise composition of tribal population confirms

---

1 Dr. Eyingbeni Hümtsoe-Nienu teaches Christian Theology and HoD of the Department of Christian Theology, Clark Theological College, Mokokchung, Nagaland.

this; Assam – 12.4%, Arunachal Pradesh – 68.8%, Nagaland – 86.5%, Meghalaya – 86.1%, Tripura – 31.8%, Mizoram – 94.4%, Manipur – 35.1% and Sikkim – 33.8%.[2] A common strand of worldview evident among the tribals in the region is the idea of cosmic interdependence. This idea can be put into context to achieve solidarity and harmony among and across different religions. The sense of cosmic interdependence contributes to raising one's level of being a part of the greater whole. Religious affinity notwithstanding, there are dimensions in the tribal primal worldview[3] that challenges humanity to rethink their relationship with one another and with the rest of creation.

In this essay, I have used indigenous/tribal primal worldview as a framework to achieve dual purposes; to firstly draw trans-religious/universal values from it and secondly to reformulate a perspective for inter-religious harmony. The approach evidenced is phenomenological in that I have chosen to focus on the 'essence'[4] of primal tribal worldview.

Nuances of Cosmic Interdependence in Tribal Primal Worldview

Unity of Life in the Supreme Being, the Creator

The Sovereignty of God is not a contentious topic among religions. This reality is the chief foundation of tribal primal belief. The Supreme Being as Potsow (Lotha), Tsüngrem (Ao), Alhou (Sümi), Pathian/Khuanu (Mizo), Kepenoufü (Angami), Tatara Rabunga (Achik),[5] etc., is the cosmic Creator.[6] The primal conception of

2 "Demographic Status of Scheduled Tribe Population of India," tribal.nic.in/demographic.pdf (accessed 14/10/2016).

3 By "worldview" I simply mean a people's way of looking at life in its totality.

4 Cf., John V. Matthew, *Theories and Methods in the Study of Religions: Philosophico-Theological Appraisal based on Socio-Psychological & Subaltern Concerns* (New Delhi: CWI, 2016), 24ff.

5 These are the proper names of God in different tribal languages.

6 Eyingbeni Hümtsoe-Nienu, *God of the Tribes: Christian Perspective on the Naga Ancestral Idea of the Supreme Being* (Mokokchung, NL: CTC, 2014), 75ff.

God's relationship with creation contrasts with dualism, monism and even pantheism.[7] The non-dualist, non-monist, non-pluralist posture of the relationship between God and creatures can be described in the words of Spanish-Indian theologian Panikkar, "God is neither Same (monism) nor the Other (dualism). God is one pole of reality, a constitutive pole. This pole is nothing in itself. It exists only in its polarity, in its relationship. God is relationship, intimate internal relationship with all."[8] The Khasi concept of the unity between created beings and Creator offers a meaningful summation. Juanita War, Professor of Linguistics at NEHU, asserts that "the ancient Khasis recognized the unity of life, there is no division between different forms of life since all are inclusive under one 'body' and all are equally subject to *Ka Hok* and *Ka Hukum Blei*[9] [who] enfolds both humans and nature within his loving arms."[10]

The Justice of God

God as the impartial judge of all humans and their deeds is woven into primal thought and belief. This idea prompted our progenitors to; first, trust God implicitly and second, rely on his judgment explicitly. The acknowledgement of the Sovereignty of God and human's inevitable accountability to God ensured that socio-economic-civil and religious justice was done to all citizens of the village/tribe. The consciousness of divine retribution over those who exceeded norms (Lothas call it *tsoyakvoyak*[11]) was deemed as a just retribution of the omniscient God. Traditional legal proceedings, at times, appear to have been conducted under open skies in the presence of the Supreme Being, who dispensed the final verdict, accepted without the need to oppose. Smith, a

7 Cf., Raimon Panikkar, *The Experience of God: Icons of the Mystery*, Trans. Joseph Cunneen (Minneapolis, MN: Fortress, 2006), 62.

8 *Ibid.*, 63.

9 Both terms are Khasi expressions of the Creator God.

10 Juanita War, "The Khasi Concept of Nature," *The Tribal Worldview and Ecology*, eds. A. Wati Longchar and Yangkahao Vashum (Jorhat, AS: TSC, 1998), 43.

11 It literally means "doing or going beyond" the norm in a negative way.

sociologist and missionary to the Nagas recounts such instances one of which is recorded as follows;

> If one man calls another a thief, but the charge is denied, the accused may be requested to bite a tiger's tooth or to place his hand on the tiger's skull and repeat these words; "I have done no wrong, I have not stolen from this man's house. May the sun and moon smite me if I have done wrong". After this oath the elders proceed to count his hogs, fowl, cattle, dogs and other possessions. Should anything disappear or should any misfortune befall him within a certain time, his guilt would be established and the fine be levied.[12]

Likewise, offences against fellow human beings and other creatures that resulted in loss of life (homicide or fatal diseases), disruption of regular lifecycles (thunder and storm) and paranormal occurrences (famine and drought) are treated as manifestation of God's wrath and displeasure in erring humans. Since, God is conceived as infallible, whatever consequences befall the village, they simply make peace with it. Appeasement strategy works only in relation to spirits – the lesser beings and not the Supreme Being. This is so because God only demands obedience and just behaviors from humans.

The Non-autonomy of Creation

The principle of the non-autonomy of creation runs through the entirety of primal worldview. As much as creation shares commonality in being created by the Creator, they are also indispensably connected to one another in their bond of life. Primal tribal religion is characterized by belief in ubiquitous presence of spirits, leading to wrongful naming of their religion as animism. The idea that human beings are anything but sovereign and autonomous is squashed by their submission to the demands of supernatural beings in return for bountiful harvest, games, health, peace and progeny. This relationship is not of unity in the monistic sense but rather of inter-connectness that affirms

12 William C. Smith, *The Ao Naga Tribe of Assam* (Delhi: Mittal, 2002 [1925]), 62 cited in Eyingbeni Hümtsoe-Nienu, *God of the Tribes*, 120-21.

that reality of all sorts are not isolated or segregated from each other. Lycanthropy affirms the correlation between animals and humans. Birds and other creatures render identity and service of appeasement to end political hostilities and heal illnesses. Likewise, as pointed out by Nienu, "In the Naga tradition, nature is the arena in which the supernatural realms and human world intersects."[13] This connectivity is regenerated by the observance of *genna*[14] that involves introspection by way of ceasing all activity and leading to rejuvenation of all aspects and forms of life for a fresh beginning.[15]

Humans as Relational Beings in Community

The idea of an absolute individual would appall traditional tribal minds. What is inherent in Buddhist philosophy and psychology is also embedded in tribal view. Thurman points out that in Buddhism the 'individual' is a 'living, relative, social, conventional being' and that there is no such things as an unchanging, ultimate, isolated and an intrinsically identifiable 'individual.'[16] Humans derive meaning in relation to community life. Being a person means being a part of a greater whole. When a person commits grave error, one is deprived of this privilege or right by way of isolation/ expulsion – whether it's a temporary or a permanent one. Other culpable offenses are paid off with in kind. Those who are mentally unable to take responsibility – like minor and psychiatric patients – rightly find exception – but not their guardians.[17] Lovely is correct in pointing out the many hierarchical 'ideals' in traditional tribal systems that defy the essence of communitarianism on the

---

13 V. Nienu, *Naga Cultural Milieu: AN Adaptation to Mountain Ecosystem* (San Francisco, CA: Dorylus, 2015), 150.

14 Derived from Tenyidie word *Kenyü* meaning "taboo/prohibition".

15 Eyingbeni Humtsoe-Nienu, Paul Pimomo and Venusa Tunyi, *Nagas: Essays for Responsible Change* (Dimapur, NL: Heritage, 2012), 90-91.

16 Robert A. F. Thurman, "Social and Cultural Rights in Buddhism," *Human Rights and the World's Religions*, ed., Leroy S. Rouner (Notre Dame, IN: University of Notre Dame, 1988), 150.

17 N. Talitemjen Jamir and A. Lanunungsang, *Naga Society and Culture* (Lumami, NL: NU, Tribal Research Centre, 2005), 60-61; Cf., 59-73.

basis particularly of class and gender[18] and also with regards to individual freedom. However, this does not nullify the value of community life that, at times, was the only foundation of survival for the weak, the poor, the sick, dead and the dying. The tribal primal community system, although not perfect, when especially viewed from gender perspective, generally recognizes a person's need of the community and the community's duty towards the wellbeing of a person. The relation between people within a village community takes importance above relationship between different clans and genealogy. Visitors to the community also are treated with respect. Harming them is liable to penalty.[19] Thus, the importance of relationality with all peoples is affirmed.

Earth as a Common Habitat and Source of Sustenance for Creation

As people that depend on natural resources for sustenance, primal tribals view the ecosphere as connected to existence itself. A new sense of 'deep ecology' as an 'ethical and religious attitude' of valuing nature for its own sake and seeing it as divine or spiritually vital[20] has emerged among world religions. The success of 19th century anthropocentric evangelical missionary theology meant the erosion of indigenous values connected with entirety of life around the axis of the Supreme Being. V. Nienu rightly opines that for Naga tribals, Earth – "contains all the valuable things people must learn and master – mountains, hills, forests, rivers, valleys and all the ecological resources that each represents. Earth is the habitat for the animals, insects, birds, fish, tress and grasses, for food and for every need.[21] Nature also provided tools for agriculture, clothing, and crafts (basketry, pottery), weapons,

18 Lovely Awomi James, *Tribal Theology: Reviewing the Naga Traditional Worldview* (New Delhi: CWI, 2017), 106-111.

19 *Ibid.*, 61.

20 David Landis Barnhill and Roger S. Gottlieb, "Introduction", *Deep Ecology and World Religions: New Essays on Sacred Ground*, eds., David Landis Barnhill and Roger S. Gottlieb (Albany, NY: State University of NY, 2001), 1, cf., 5-8.

21 V. Nienu, *Naga Cultural Milieu*, 140-41.

toys, means of transportation and healthcare. It is also the inspiration for songs, proverbs, legends and myths. The continuity of tribal communities is clearly linked to their collective sense of dependence on earth as their home, teacher, playground, doctor, and most of all another – who procreates, nurtures, sustains life and beyond - in the land of the dead.

Significance of Primal Idea of Cosmic Interdependence for Interreligious Harmony

In her essay, 'Interfaith Dialogue: Contribution of Traditional Nagas', Mary Chang has identified 'points of contact' whereby traditional Naga religion and other faiths can meet and develop a new form of inter-faith spirituality.[22] The novelty of such objective, drawn from traditional religion, is noteworthy. However, I intend to establish significance of primal tribal idea for religious harmony not by suggesting a need for 'meeting points' but for drawing inspiration from primal worldview in order to challenge religious attitudes and practices that contribute to destruction of human relations and non-human lives.

Intra-religious Humility

The basic universal idea of cosmic-interdependence leaves no room for any religion to claim itself as the *Sanadhana dharma* - the highest religion or as being the crown of religions. Inherent in the scheme of cosmic interdependence is the presumption that no religion or religious adherent can make claims of solitary absoluteness, separated from other religions. There is a need for the practice of humility that changes attitude towards other religions and towards one's own religion as well. This practice of humility is to be marked by two levels of attitudinal posturing; Submission to the Sovereignty of the One God and resting from intra-religious arrogance of self-sufficiency.

22 Cf., Mary Chang, "Interfaith Dialogue: Contribution of Traditional Nagas," *Doing Theology with Indigenous People's Spirituality*, eds., R. Sashikaba Kechutzar and Zulunungsang Lemtur (Jorhat/Mokokchung/Kolkatta: TSC, CCPRA, SCEPTRE, 2016), 120-131.

Cosmic relationship centered on the Supreme Being pulls people of all religions towards a central matrix of the Divine. This God is Absolute and yet is not a solitary monad. Such realization ought to propel people to accept their unity in God, by whatever name known. Religious parochialism, informed by false sense of supremacy over the 'other' disrupts not only one's relationship with God but also with each other. The consequence of which would have to be accepted as divine retribution for creatures failing to live in harmony with each other. The wisdom for need of the 'other' requires acknowledging that in God all things are bound together to make a complete whole.

It would be far-fetched to identify Community (Thanzuava, 1997), land (Wati Longchar, 2000) or Kinship (Lalpekhlua, 2007) as a basis of tribal life because one of the premises can be entirely used to bring religions together. At least in the context of interfaith relations and dialogue, the specificity of emphasis on a people group, space and ancestry has more potential to separate than to unite. The one credible basis of life that can successfully pull religions into one accord is God, before whom religious imperialism becomes a mockery of God's immensity. As the Creator, the Supreme Beings shows no favoritism for creation, irrespective of religions, since they are all God's beloved children.

Mutual Enrichment through Peaceable Conduct

No religion is inherently evil and pursuance of destructive behavior contradicts any religious ideal of peace and harmony. But adherents of a religion can be both evil and hence destructive. Also, institutionalized religious boundaries isolate peoples and nations. No good can ever come out from a place where there is no mutually enriching system that cuts across religions, with its multi-layered identities such as race, ethnicity, caste, class, etc. In primal tribal thought, the argument for a private faith or private person would be a delirious utterance. The Lotha Nagas have this to say – "What is the use of 'One'?" Such rhetorical may not imply the worthlessness of an individual but of the weakness of a single entity – even if that entity were a group of a ghettoized nature.

Adherents of any religion have to be conscious of the peace of the community at large. Fanaticism does not do that. As much as God is a relational being, people of all religions benefit most by being open to each other. The primal tribal puts value to the ideal of selflessness. The Mizos' recognition of *tlawmngaihna* as foundational to effective social existence operates obviously on the principle of 'welfare for all.'[23] Since humanity is meant to be communitarian, creating religious microcosm by way of isolating themselves is a loss for the isolating religion as well as those religions that would've benefited greatly from openness with an aim to sharing the rich array of resources that every religion brings to the table. A global community is possible when religions are instructed by the truth that we are responsible for each other to improve each other's lives and become respectable ambassadors of our faith.

As part of the global community, professing different religions need not cause separation between fellow beings. The common human identity must be preserved and defended at all cost to ensure that the human community and the journey of the members therein find support that everyone plays their part of the *Good Samaritan* (Luke 10:25-37). Excesses towards one another in the basis of religious affiliation will certainly invite disharmony and ultimately the displeasure of God – manifested in various ways that can be deemed the just retribution of God.

Collective Commitment to Inclusive Coexistence

American environmentalists, Barnhill and Gottliebaccuses religious traditions for their role in creating an ecological disaster and that they were 'pretty much blind to the environmental crisis until it was pointed out to them by other [poets and philosophers]' and laments that it was not the voices of ministers, priests, popes or rabbis.[24] To the list can be added - of Imams, pundits, gurus and

23 For the varied meanings and implications of the word, see K. Thanzauva, *Theology of Community: Tribal Theology in the Making* (Aizawl, MZ: Author for Mizo Theological Conference, 1997), 120-123.

24 Barnhill and Gottlieb, "Introduction", *Deep Ecology*, 2-3.

monks. It appears that leaders of the world religions have been at the receiving end of not addressing environmental crises, but adherents of each religion are equally culpable. Again, no religion per endorses human right to abuse the non-human domain but its faithfuls have found a way to gobble up the natural resources because of capitalistic appetite. American ethicist, Rasmussen accuses Homo sapiens' tendency to live as though we constituted an ecologically segregated species. The result is 'species apartheid'. One 'race' – the human race – subjugates the rest of the biosphere for human benefit alone.[25]

The non-human world obviously is less dependent on humanity for survival as we are to it. In connecting with the non-human world without pride and greed, humanity learns that religious differences resulting in negative consequences are a hindrance to our inter-relational coexistence. We will do better if we were to embrace the fact that earth is our only home (for now) and that it provides and nourishes us. Nature does not discriminate anyone on the basis of religious affiliation. If we are good to it, it will continue to sustain us. On the other hand, human instigated conflicts result in unrest for the entire cosmos. Tragically, humanity's aggressiveness towards fellow beings usually extends to the non-human world. Conflicts arising out of religion-based enmity or religious profiling have adverse repercussions on the natural habitat in which we exist. Humanity is a witness to indiscriminate destruction of nature and environment as a result of human conflicts; a sure sign that human conflict impacts nature and creates a vicious cycle of mutual destruction. Making peace between religions safeguards their collective wellbeing in relation to environment and simultaneously contributes to preserving the dignity of nature – the handiwork of God – and consequently ensuring peace and harmony between people.

---

25 Larry Rasmussen, "Introduction – Eco-Justice: Church and Community Together," *Earth Habitat: Eco-Justice and the Church's Response*, eds. Dieter Hessel and Larry Rasmussen (Minneapolis: MN: Fortress, 2001), 1.

Conclusion

Indigenous primal worldview may not provide a foolproof remedy for establishing inter-religious and intra-religious harmony. However, the essence of tribal worldview, when invoked into our present world, can very well transform relationships and provide defenses for the need to cooperate and coexist. Today, the world, more than even beckons religions to turn less fanatic and become more accepting of each other. It's to any religion's peril to presume that isolated existence is possible or even beneficial. The walls erected on grounds of superiority are best dismantled realizing that at the end of the day, we are one in God, in our humanity, our habitat and natural resources. The importance of maintaining the cosmic chain of interdependence need to be reaffirmed by people of all religions, believing that when any part of the chain snaps the potentiality of destruction is also of cosmic proportion. The knowledge of cosmic interdependence, provided by primal tribal worldview, is a valuable perspective to keep our relationship with God and all else not only meaningful but also productive.

5

Problems and Challenges of Living in a Religiously Plural World Theo-Ethical Consideration

Rongsen Longkumer[1]

Religious pluralism is a reality of the modern world. It provides an opportunity for many people for greater exchange between different traditions and to some, extend appreciation of faiths and traditions that are different from one's own. If we want to agree with K.C. Abraham who says that multi-religious situations enriches our life and relationships.[2] Therefore, it is affirmed that the future lies not in destroying or suppressing the particularities of our diverse religious heritage, but in finding non-hegemonic ways to celebrate them.[3]

Conceptualization for the Terms

Religious Pluralism

Religious pluralism is the term used for the unity in diversity. It is the life-together of people of different faiths. It is a reality which

---

1 Rev. Dr. Rongsen Longkumer, Professor of Christian Ethics at Clark Theological College, Mokokchung till 2016.

2 K.C. Abraham, *Transforming Vision* (Thiruvalla: CSS, 2006), p. 271.

3 James, Athius, *Towards an Ethics of Community* (Ontario, Canada: Canada Cooperation for Studies, N.D), 200.

affirmed that humanity is one, though they are divided by their various religious/cultural experiences.[4]

R. Panikkar explained that the different religious traditions of humankind are like almost indefinite number of colors that appear as the divine or simply white light of reality that falls on the prism of human existence. It affirms that reality is one though it appears as different.[5] According to Samartha, the term Religious pluralism is a heavy academic concept which should be broken open to reveal the vast number of people and the faith they live by. It refers to millions of people and neighbors of other faiths who share the common life or community with us.[6] Pluralism of religions is seemed primarily as a pluralism of human relationships, which we would think is inevitable.[7] There is a universal acceptance of the concept of pluralism. It is rightly affirmed that plurality belongs to the very structure of reality. Religious pluralism is a fact of life. It needs to be affirmed and celebrated. That is the only way to achieve and the only mode of practicing pro-existence in a multi-religious context.[8] K.C. Abraham again argues that religious pluralism is not only a fact of life, but a value to be cherished and nurtured.[9]

Posing Problems and Challenges

Scholars are of the opinions that religious pluralism, however laudable and necessary is also a problem because of the conflicts arising out of religious differences. Demonic forces masquerading as religious loyalty is destroying the fabric of civil society in many countries. In India the clashes between Hindus and Muslims centered on religion and its sacred places cost many innocent lives.

---

4 M. Stephen, *A New Mission Agenda* (Delhi: ISPCK, 2007), p. 2.

5 R. Panikkar, *The Inter-religious Dialogue* (Bangalore: ATC, 1984), p. 25.

6 Samartha, *Courage for Dialogue* (New York: Orbis Books, 1981), p. 89.

7 M. Amaladoss, S.J., "Theological Basis for Religious Pluralism- Its Cultural Expression and Justification for its acceptance" in Arulsamy, *Communalism in India* (Bangalore: Claretian Publications, 1988), p. 124.

8 K.C. Abraham, *Transforming Vision, op.cit.,* p. 231.

9 *Ibid.*, p. 272.

The situation may continue to be tense even in the future. It is evidently clear that religious conflicts are not about doctrines and beliefs, but quite often they are triggered by social and economic factors. The control of resources, political power and the fear of losing one's group's hegemony contributes to a great deal to the conflict.[10]

The lack of openness and understanding of the religious leaders lead to mistrust, conflicts and suspicion which prevents the meaningful dialogical existence and relationships. They draw a sharp line between themselves and people of other faiths as 'the saved' and the 'damned.'[11]

It is the view of Samartha that despising the religions of other people as devilish, nonsense and good for nothing and claiming superiority to one's own religion can sometimes be a form of racism which generates hatred and conflicts.[12]

M. Stephen argues that one of the main problems in the context of religious pluralism is the claims and the counterclaims in the name of religious leaders. Each religion claims that their religion is true and their Guru is the unique and Universal Savior. This gives rise to conflicts and disharmony. This kind of claim can lead the people of particular faiths to be imperialistic and condemnatory over others. The emphasis on the one and the only is not to be appreciated in the pluralistic context.[13]

It is the opinion of Paul Knitter that in any situation of a healthy religious pluralism, identity of different religions should be preserved. However we need to reject all absolute claims in the name of identity. All ethno-centric programs distort the web of human relationships. We envisage a pluriform community of communities this comes as a big challenge to the hegemonising tendency to globalization.[14]

---

10 *Ibid.*, p. 274.

11 M. Stephen, *op.cit.*, p. 85.

12 Samartha, *Courage for Dialogue*, p. 89.

13 M. Stephen, *op.cit.*, p. 28.

14 Paul Knitter, "Cosmic Preferential option" in *Bangalore Theological Forum*, Vol. XXIII, No. 4, December 1991, p. 23.

Almost all the problems are related to our understanding and practice of mission. In this sense, what Samartha has said is right. He said that the traditional concept of Mission was characterized by the negative attitude towards the people of other faiths. This negative attitude towards mission was shaped by the colonial era, its Europe dominated history, church centered theology and unexamined assumptions of western superiority of races, culture and religion. Thus mission has been absurd and had doubtful methods.[15]

K.C. Abraham strongly argues that mission should not be directed towards the conquest of a pagan culture and satanic religions. Mission, as it is affirmed, is the witness of a community of faith to God's transformation act through Jesus Christ. Mission is not an aggressive propaganda but a way of life. It is solidarity with people, especially with the suffering people.[16]

M. Stephen believes that the traditional evangelical understanding of mission to other faiths is antagonistic, conflictual, confrontational, provocative, judgmental and exclusive. They do not see any good value in other religious traditions. Thus their approach to other religions is very intolerant and aggressive. Everyone has their right to present their faith or ideology or the goodness of their Guru, but it should not be presented in an irritative manner, without condemning other faiths and without hurting other's sentiments, one can follow his/her own religion and present the gospel of God.[17]

R. Panikkar also argues that in order to avoid conflicts and misunderstanding, cosmic Christ should not be presented in an irritating and provocative manner. We could present the person and his/her message in a very appealing way without compromising our faith and without compromising our Guru with that of others. What we need is presenting the love of Christ which makes Him

---

15 Samartha, *Courage for Dialogue*, *op.cit.*, p. 79.

16 K.C. Abraham, *Liberative Solidarity* (Thiruvalla: CSS, 2006), p. 14.

17 M. Stephen, *op.cit.*, p. 83.

unique. We are not supposed to bring hostility among people in the name of the uniqueness of our Guru.[18]

P.D. Devananda believed that 'encounter' and 'confrontation' are not the ways to present the gospel. The provocative statements are to be avoided. There should not be arrogance and exclusive claims in the presentation of the gospel.[19] When criticizing the traditional concept and practice of mission, Samartha expressed that to be in mission is not to undermine and destroy other religions. He rejected the missiology of conquest. He was critical of the military terminologies like, pioneer, campaign and the demonic elements in the colonialist ideas which distorted the true understanding of the Christian mission.[20]

When how to avoid creating problems in the presentation of gospel Fr. Paul Puthanagady says that in proclamation of the gospel we have to take into account the other person's sensibility, view point and mental structure, while in affirmation it is enough that the statement is logically correct and based on documentary evidences. A refined concept of mission and evangelism includes to create brotherhood/sisterhood of humanity and communal harmony. In order to do this, we require a proper understanding of others not only in terms of their religious belief, but in terms of their concrete life situation.[21]

In the opinion of K.C. Abraham, if we accept a pluralistic framework in our relationships with other faiths, our mission concepts and practice ought to undergo a drastic change. We need to move away from a triumphant model of mission to a solidarity model. Mission is God's mission of life-giving. Therefore, our mission is to discern God's act and testify to it in our lives.[22]

---

18 R. Panikkar, quoted by M. Stephen, *op.cit.,* p. 29.

19 P.D. Devananda, quoted by M. Stephen, *op. cit.*, p. 48.

20 Samartha, *Courage for Dialogue*, *op.cit.,* p. 79.

21 Fr. Puthanangady, "Communalism a Theological Reflection" in Arulsamy ed., *Communalism in India, op.cit.*, p. 161.

22 K.C. Abraham, *Transforming Vision*, *op. cit.,* p. 281.

Theo-ethical Response

Ethics is reflection on the basis of moral action. For instance, why I ought to do, what I ought to do? Ethics is a reflective and scientific study. In simplest sense, 'Theology means what we believe and 'Ethics' means why we believe'. Peter C. Phan argues that God is not an exclusive God and is at work in all communities to save them. Christ is working in all people to enlighten them and to lead them to the ultimate truth. God is revealing himself in other religions but everyone does not acknowledge or recognize it. Since God is active in history, His revelation is found everywhere and it can be sensed. As God through Christ is working in all other mysterious ways, God in Christ can be experienced in all religious traditions.[23]

R. Panikkar also argued that even before the very incarnation of God, He was working in history and even today He is still at work. We should not limit Him as the 'Jesus of Nazareth' alone, but also as the universal one who is active in the whole cosmos regardless of religions and races. There is a transcendental dimensions of Christ who is imminent in the life of the whole humanity.[24]

It is the view of Ernst Troeltsch that no religion can claim to be the full and final realization of the divine presence. Truth will have always many cultural expressions and it is impossible to judge one to be better that the other.[25]

It is also the opinion of John Hick that the different religions are different streams of religious experience; each having began at a different point within human historyand each having formed its own conceptual self-consciousness within a different cultural milieu. Therefore, religious experiences are also plural. He also

---

23 Peter C. Phan, "The Claim of Uniqueness and Universality" in *Inter-faith Dialogue Indian Theological Studies*, Vol. XXI, No. 1, March 1994, p. 9.

24 R. Panikkar, quoted by M. Stephen, p. 42.

25 Ernst Troeltsch, quoted by Paul Knitter in No Other Name, Phillippines Claretian Publications, 1985, pp. 21, 31.

believed that great world religions as different human response to the one same divine reality.[26]

In the opinion of M. Amaladoss that diversity is not due to human limitation or sin, but it is a gift of God. Since God is an omnipresent God, He is never absent; He may be present in various manners or degrees or with varying efficacy. The plan of God for the world is one and it is the same God who is present and active to bring this plan to a fulfillment in history. Diversity may arise from many sources as the plan of God. The human persons who receive such a revelation perceive it and express it from their limited personal, social, religious, historical and cultural point of view. Therefore, it is affirmed that a deeper cause for diversity could be God's own plan to communicate Himself in a variety of ways not only to manifest the richness of His being, but also to take into account the cultural and historical diversity arising out of the freedom and creativity that are His own gifts to humanity. He also said that every religion while it is different from others is also limited, not because of the reality that it mediates on and makes present in, but because of its capacity to experience and to express is limited, because human capacity to experience is not only limited but also ambiguous. Apart from this fact, human beings are historically, culturally and humanly limited above all it is also sinful.[27]

M. Amaladoss strongly argues that pluralism of religions is seen primarily as a pluralism of relationships, which we would think is inevitable. Even where Christ is not visibly acknowledged, His spirit continues his hidden work and leads all things to unity. He believes that Christ is not only Jesus, Christ may also be mediated by other symbols in other religious traditions. While acknowledging the other possibilities of other symbols and mediations of Christ, the specificity of Jesus as the humanity of Christ is also strongly affirmed. God reaches out to every human

---

26 John Hick, *Philosophy of Religion* (New Delhi: Prentice Hall India Ltd., 1988), pp. 115, 142.

27 M. Amaladoss, "Theological Basis for Religious Pluralism," *op.cit.*, pp. 118-120.

person in ways unknown to us. For a particular person the way in which God is actually reaching out to him/her historically is the best way. From this point of view, comparing ways among themselves is totally pointless. Precisely because God's mystery is universal and as such His manifestation itself is also universal and in a variety of ways, no one's manifestation can claim to ultimacy.[28]

Basing in the firm foundation of theology of pluralism, George V. Lobo S.J expresses that communalism is corruption of community, essentially religious communities. It is the mobilization and politicization of religious groups organized on the basis of powerful symbols to fight for narrow goals. It is highly responsible on the part of communal and religious leaders to play on the religious feelings of the masses and make them victims of communal conflicts. When power brokers play the communal game, the whole population is manipulated and democracy is reduced to mockery. It is generally the poor people who suffer the most and have to bear the brunt of the periodic bouts of violence that arises. The rich and powerful incite violence, but do not take active part in mob violence and hence do not have to suffer from the attack of rival groups or security forces. Conflicts are started in the name of justice and human rights of religious freedom. But behind such slogans, there is naked self-interest. Appeal is made to the sense of self-sacrifice for a noble cause. But often the hidden agenda was for killing and destruction. Such immoral acts and behaviors need to be denounced in the strongest language. It is criminal to exploit socio-economic imbalances to provoke communal riots. The attempts to fight socio-economic injustices should not lead to further deterioration of the situation particularly when the struggle is given a communal tone. It is wrong to kill hundreds of 'living temples of God' for the sake of defending the sanctity of a handmade temple.

Sacredness of human life is more valuable and important that the sacredness of anything else because the human person alone is made in the image of God and all other signs of God are

28 *Ibid.*, pp. 124, 129.

of only relative value. There is meaningless in the blessings and consecration of sacred places and objects. In any dispute regarding such things, the paramount dignity and rights of the human being should not be lost sight of.[29]

In the opinion of Ucko, as time continues to enfold the complexities of life, life itself becomes even more apparent that old models do not always suffice. The other needs to remain other in his/her integrity to the entire truth, that we need the other in order to fathom more. We are not helped by others becoming us or confirming us. He quoted Rabbi of Kolzk, who said, "If I am I and you are you, because you are you, then I am I and you are you. But if I am I because you are you, and you are you because I am I, then I am not I and you are not you". No human being is an island. Every human being needs to relate to the other, to others and to a community. Religious fundamentalism and its traditions today hinder the formation of a new community. There is a tendency toward mono cultures threatening the mosaics of religious plurality and an open human community. It is in such an unmerciful environment, that destructive and violent force and hatred and lust for power emerges and takes over. Although, different from each other and functioning on various levels, they are all intertwined and are obstacles to the development of human wellbeing and building a new community. Community of communities is not an entity in and by itself, but relational and open in nature. It has no boundaries but exist as an organic relationship spontaneous and creative. People of different faiths have specific and distinctive contributions to make the new community, provided they are given space for their own integrity and identity. No one should be the object of the other. We are interchangeably subject and object, I and thou. There are enough possibilities to builda new community provided we are willing

29 George Lobo S.J., "Ethical and Religious Dimensions of Communalism" in Arulsamy, ed., *Communalism in India, Ibid.*, pp. 164-165.

to accept others as they are. The context of plurality obliges an openness that goes beyond our own confine.[30]

Samartha believes that to reject exclusivism and to accept plurality, to be committed to our one's faith and to be open to the faith commitment of our neighbor is to live in a global community of communities, sharing the ambiguities of history and the mystery of life which are the imperatives of our modern age.[31]

Paul Knitter argues that our criterion for judging what is 'true or false', 'good or bad' is no longer 'is it in the scripture' but rather 'does it remove human sufferings and promote life.'[32] In the view of K.C. Abraham the Trinity is unity in community. According to it, each divine person penetrates the other and allows himself/herself to be penetrated, yet each maintains his/her own identity and sharing community. Unity of equal partners bound by mutual love is a model that expresses divine reality. Our relationship in the socio-religious groups should follow this model. Plurality expresses this reality. Each assimilates the other without destroying the identity of the other. Pluriform unity is the glorious celebration of the Triune God. Therefore, any system or ideology that is used to protect one's own vested interest at the exclusion of the other distorts God's purpose for humanity. On the other hand, the relationship based on plurality and unity that allows different identities to co-exist can be a humble expression of the mystery of holy trinity.[33]

In the words of Lynn A. De Selva that all people are of equal significance to God, God has no favorites and he has no partiality. He quotes that the people of Israel are like people of Sudan to me, I brought Philistine from Crete, Syrians from Kir, just as I brought Israel from Egypt. Thus says the Lord (Amos 9:7); Therefore, the

30 Han Ucko, "Interfaith Dialogue: Ethical Consideration Towards Building New Communities" in Daniel Chetti and M.P. Josephin, *Ethical Issues in the Struggle for Justice* (Thiruvalla: CSS, 1998), pp. 13, 19.

31 Samartha, "Globalization and its Cultural Consequences" in Daniel Chetti and M.P. Joseph, ed., *Ethical Issues in the Struggle for Justice*, *Ibid.*, p. 193.

32 Paul Knitter, "Cosmic Preferential option" in Bangalore Theological Forum, *op.cit.*, p. 23.

33 K.C. Abraham, *Transforming Vision, op.cit.*, p. 281.

exodus event does not give the Jewish people a special privilege or status. Peter learns, perhaps for the first time that the religious laws set by religious traditions are not the boundaries within which God operates. Such religious laws are often necessary and they help provide identity, coherence and meaning for particular religious communities (Corleluis story- Acts 10). God is spirit and those who worships Him must worship Him in spirit and truth (Jn 4:21ff); that means the Spirit of God cannot be privatized or localized. Paul's speech in Aerophague (Acts 17) was a good example of his respect and recognition to the people of other faiths. He appreciated the sense of worship among the people and then quoted from their own literature and presented Jesus Christ without hurting the sentiments of the others (Acts 17).[34]

Let us conclude in this way that religion provides the deepest inspiration for human mortality. But when the religious sentiment goes astray, it has to be regulated by mortality. This aberrations like that of caste and exploitation of the followers by religious leaders, making them subservient to their selfish interest, fatalism, obscurantisms and fanaticism, have to be judged according to the norms and values of mortality which are manifested by scriptures, conscience and human reasons.[35]

---

34 Lynn A. DeSelva, "The Theological Significance of People of Other Faiths" in C.D. Jathana, ed., *Dialogue in Community* (Mangalore: KATHRI, 1982), p. 31.

35 George Lobo, S.J., "Ethical and Religious Dimension of Communalism" *op.cit.*, p. 162.

6

Concept of 'the Other' in the Mind-set of Contemporary Hindus

***Prabhakar Bhattacharyya*[1]**

"Om! Sahanāvavatu; Sahanaubhunaktu; Sahaviryamkaravavahai; Tejusvinavadhītamastu; Mā, vidvisāvahai; Om; Sāntiḥ, Sāntiḥ, Sāntiḥ." (Om! May He (God) protect us both! May He be pleased with us! With Vigour may we work together! Successful may our study be! Let us not hate one another! Om! Peace! Peace! Peace!) Religion or faith having tremendous public implications cannot be treated just as a private matter of individuals. Though religious pluralism is a fact throughout the ages, controversial issues cannot be avoided in any interreligious dialogue. Hence, all the parties involved should come forward with open mind to work together. "The intuitive apprehension of unity in diversity is one of the fundamental characteristic of Indian mind. This consciousness of the manifold phenomena converging on a central point which gives them reality and life is essentially the religious experience. So, the distinctive feature of the Indian character can be called religiousness. In fact in India, configuration of moral values, the religious value is the common centre of the various concentric circles representing the other values. Even today, when the streams of religious consciousness in the minds of the orthodox turns into

---

1 Dr. Prabhakar Bhattacharyya is Associate Professor & Head Philosophy Department, Serampore College.

a stagnant pool and in the modern educated into a shallow brook, the religious impulse is so strong that one can neither think of a philosophy of life which is not based on religion."[2] "It is [the] realization of the Absolute, swiping away the distinction between 'I' and 'Thou' which is the central idea in the religious philosophy of the Hindus and which is to them the ultimate moral value."[3]

All incarnations, prophets and saints of Hinduism reconfirm through their own experience the famous Vedic revelation that, 'God is theone and only reality, scholars ascribe different names' (*ekam sat vipra bahudha vadanti*). Hinduism maintains that different religions are simply different paths, leading to the same goal, i.e., God or the Absolute. So, theoretically, there cannot be any 'other' to be converted within its fold. The present paper is humble attempt to understand the concept of 'the other' in the 'mind-set' of the contemporary Hindus.

'Mind-set' generally means an individual's totality of belief about life and reality. In fact, 'mind-set' represents one's personal view of the world and how one interprets it. 'Mind-set' sometimes means 'A way of thinking or attitude or opinion, specially a habitual one.' In a broad sense, it is a general philosophy or view of life.'Mind-set' varies from person to person; time, place, economic, cultural, educational and religious background play an immense role in moulding one's mind-set. Throughout the process of education, change in 'Mind-set' is possible. But for common adult house-holders change of mind-set is a rare phenomenon. Characteristics of 'Mind-set' can be inferred from one's spontaneous talk and habitual public behaviour.

Hinduism as a religious tradition is at least four thousand years old. This tradition had to undergo many shocks through the ages. Many Hindus converted to Buddhism, Jainism, Christianity, Islam, Sikhism, and other religions. The Hindu tradition survived even after 'convert or kill' waves from the invaders. The tradition survives because of arrival of great saints and sages in different

---

2 Husain, S. Abid, *The National Culture of India*, National Book Trust, India, New Delhi, 1978, p. 176.

3 *Ibid.*, p. 177.

centuries who moulded the mind-set of the then Hindus for not only tolerance but also acceptance of 'the others', be those foreigners or converts.

The policy of universal acceptance is often taunted by some, as Hindus pick up elements from other religions and absorb those. Then what is original? It is true that Hindus have no obligation to follow any cardinal principle to identify themselves as Hindus. In our time, Hindus live in almost all the countries of the world, and estimated number is more than 100 crores. 15% of world population is Hindu, while 31.5% is Christian and 23.2% Muslim. It is noteworthy that about 80% of Indians identify themselves as Hindus.

To identify oneself as 'Hindu' is very easy. At the time of census one has to make a self-declaration that the members of his or her family are Hindus and forefathers had such and such profession, hence be included in such and such caste or class. The author of the present paper knows some who practised religion of their parents before attaining adulthood, managed to register themselves as members of scheduled class and got certificate to that effect, from the appropriate authority.

No formal proof of conversion, reconversion or initiation is required to become a Hindu, in fact it was never required.[4] Hindus do not have any central authority to testify who is Hindu and who is not. Some politicians are trying to convince people that 'beef-eaters' are not Hindus. But the author personally knows a few 'beef-eater' Hindu politicians who are honest, enlightened, educated and sincere. In fact, in no standard Hindu scripture have I found clear prohibition against eating of cow-flesh, but it is in the mind-set of the common Hindus that as we are nourished with cow milk, we should take care of cows even when they cease to give milk, like that of an old mother who is not able to do household

---

4 Hinduism was not propagated on a particular moment of recorded history. In fact, Hindus rarely identified themselves as Hindus before 18th century, CE, Muslim rulers called non-Muslims as Hindus. Buddhist, Jains, and later Sikhs were known as Hindus. In independent India also laws regarding marriage and succession are by and large common for Hindus, Buddhists, Jains and Sikhs.

works anymore. This outlook of gratitude, a virtue is politicized in the name of religion, and becomes a vice, affecting many people. Swami Vivekananda himself, after his triumphant return from the West, met fanatics, involved in cow protection, without knowing any proper reason for their sentiment. After interesting conversation, Vivekananda depicted them as 'worthy sons of mother-cows' and exclaimed, "Who else could give birth to such accomplished children?" He actually hinted at their heartlessness towards their human brethren.[5]

Religion is a strong weapon. If the weapon is in control of narrow-minded greedy religion-mongers the result is disastrous. From my experience of interaction with religious persons of Christianity, Islam, Sikhism and other religions, I have developed the conviction that a truly religious person cannot do any harm to an individual or group belonging to other faith. But the problem is that all persons who pose to be religious are not religious. Religious identity is often highlighted to hide hypocrisy.

'Hinduism' as a religious tradition is at least four thousand years old, but its followers uses the term 'Hindu' to express their identity only for the last few centuries. Perhaps the Muslims, who ruled India from the thirteenth century, referred to all non-Muslims as Hindus. A system of faith and rituals prescribed by scripture and practiced by devout men and women are generally understood as religion. Hindus themselves call their religion *dharma* which has a wider meaning. This word is derived from the Sanskrit root '*dhr*' meaning 'to hold'. So *dharma* means to hold up the essential nature of humanity. According to traditional Hinduism, all human beings (including 'the other') are potentially divine. The task of *dharma* is to bring out that divinity.

Hinduism never had any central authority to control and regulate the lives and activities of the followers. Absolute freedom is available to all the Hindus regarding choice of the form of God or Chosen Deity (*iṣṭa*). For example, five members of a family may have five different chosen deities for worship. A Hindu may

5 Vivekananda, Swami, *The Complete Works of Swami Vivekananda*, Advaita Ashrama, Calcutta Eleventh Edition, 1985, p. 451.

also refuse all the deities and aspire the realisation of the Absolute devoid of any attribute (*Nirguṇa Brahma*).

Membership of religious organisation is only a very recent phenomenon among Hindus. Such membership is voluntary and a Hindu and even non-hindus can become a member. These organisations are cultural, social, educational and philanthropic in nature. Sometimes the term 'Mission' is used, but not involved in any type of ecumenical activities. Traditional Hinduism upheld that all religions are all right paths leading to God; the only duty is to follow one's own path with utmost sincerity. Naturally, conversion or proselytization goes against the liberal spirit of Hinduism. There is no 'other' from the spiritual outlook of the Hindus.

It is interesting to note that Hinduism upheld equal glory (potential divinity) for all humanity from the time of Vedas and Upanishads but in reality we find Hindu society is divided into many castes and classes. Even in the Rig veda, we find the mention of four varṇas, i.e., *Brahman*, *Kshatriya, Vaishya* and *Shudra.* In fact, Hindus never brought down the lofty ideal of 'potential divinity' of human beings to fit the real situation of society where people are segregated on the basis of heredity, education, wealth, merit, etc. Whatever be the birth, educational standard or economic condition ideal of 'potential divinity' is never lost. This 'ideal' is working through ages. As a result we find that saints and seers come out from any strata of social life. Once a Hindu attains 'Saint-hood', his or her heredity, profession and past life is taken into account.[6]

Traditional Hinduism, not only theoretical inclusivist, but in practical social life also rarely alienate 'the other', i.e., the people who follow different religion. Nowadays, terms like 'Aggressive Hinduism' and 'Assertive Hinduism' are very popular among politicians as well as in the religious minority. Coinage may be new, but 'Assertive' people and 'Aggressive' people

6 For example, Saint Kabir was weaver, Saint Rabidas was leather worker. Lord Sri Ramakrishna, Universally acknowledged incarnation of God, of 19th century declared that true devotees of God are above caste-class distinction.

are there among the followers of all religions. Assertive people are men or women of conviction, having adequate control over aggressiveness. These convictions come from the realization of the Truth through revelation, contemplation or reasoning, whereas aggressive people are fanatics, devoid of power of reasoning and contemplation. Shrewd fanaticizers, nowadays build image of pious persons with tactful publicity and organises huge number of fans around them. These fanaticizers want fans, not followers, as they themselves know very well that they do not possess any virtue to be imbibed by the followers. They prefer to be in the hyper-reality of cyber-space. They tweet their message, send directives through press release, living in comfort and luxury and shed tears for the down-trodden in front of camera.

Goal of Hindus is to realise God, but it is not true that all Hindus are consciously trying to achieve the goal. There are people who identify themselves as 'Hindus' but do not follow the injunctions suitable for his or her station in life. They marry with local Hindu rituals (Vedic rites sometimes); when children are born they give them Hindu names, and after death, the body is given to the funeral pyre. These people visit temples with a belief that their day-to-day misery may be reduced with the blessings of the deities.

Besides the aforesaid common Hindus there are *Pravartakas*, *Sadhakas*, *Siddhas*, and *Paramhansas*. *Pravartakas* are novitiates in the path of self realisation. It is to be noted here that in Hinduism, self-realization and God realisation is almost synonymous. *Pravatakas* search for a competent guru, get initiated with a mantra and their chosen deities are fixed for lifetime. According to their propensities as discovered by gurus, they follow the path of devotion or of action or of knowledge or of psychic control. *Sadhakas* are those who have progressed a lot in their way to self-realisation. Sadhakas hardly care for money, name or fame. In every step of life they try to depend on divine grace. Sadhakas, until they are Sidhas (realised person) avoid the company of wicked people and live a life of 'plain living and high thinking'.

Sadhakas are of two types; monastic and house-folder. There is hardly any mention of young monastic Sadhakas in the early Vedas, but the life of historical characters of Gautama Buddha and Mahavira testify that renouncing household in youth was not unknown in ancient India. However, in the Vedic scheme inhabitants of society were divided into four *varnas*. Likewise one individual's life also had four stages, namely, *brahmacharya, garhasthya, vanaprastha and sannyasa*.

From the perspective realised soul or Siddha, there cannot be any 'other', nor from the standpoint of Paramahamsa, but common people generally love a few by hating the rest. Religious organisations, political parties and sometimes even commercial institutions speak messages of love for their followers with a hidden message of hatred for 'the other'.

Einstein, the famous scientist discovered that, "Masses of people are ready to sacrifice themselves with wild enthusiasm because man has within him a lust for hatred and destruction". He asked Freud, the famous psychologist, "Is it possible to control men's mental evolution so as to make him through against the psychosis of hate and destructiveness?"[7]

Common people, who identify themselves as Hindu without caring about the goal of life and knowing almost nothing about Hinduism, are very sentimental about their identity. There is one common characteristic of all orthodox Hindus all over India is that they do not eat beef. Other marks of identity vary from place to place, caste to caste and sect to sect. There are of course many sentimental Hindus, easy prey of fanaticism, who are used by a few persons with vested earthly interest in power. Hatred is spread through public addresses; irresponsible mass media fan the flame of hatred and violence take place. Innocent people suffer and the blame goes against a particular community, even to their religion. The 'Blamc gamc' continues and hatred and counter-hatred breeds suspicion, damages trust and ultimately hamper the common good.

7 Freud replied that emphasis should be given on positive sentiment that binds humans to one another. Loving one another and developing common identification with each other may help. Distinction between leaders and followers with hierarchy of authority will however remain.

Though theoretically there cannot be 'the other' to be killed or converted, but if we seriously analyse Vedic and Puranic literature we can find some words, synonymous with 'the other'. I would like to mention a few. Those are; (1) *Mleccha* (2) *Yavana* (3) *Rakshasa* (4) *Dasas* (5) *Dasyus,* etc.

In the Rig Veda, the word 'dāsa' occurs many times, for example in 5.34.6; 6.22.10. These dāsas were originally enemies of the Vedic people and were later reduced to slavery. In some cases the term is used simply to indicate sub-ordinate persons. In the Puranic literature, 'dāsa' simply refers to a paid servant. In the contemporary Hindu society '*dāsa*' is used as a 'surname' for a person belonging to *Sudravarna*. It is interesting to note that great saints of Bhakti cult suffix their names with '*dāsa*' to mean that they are servants of God. '*Dāsya*' the 'attitude of servant' is one of the most important ways of worship for devotees. There is a famous *bhajan* by Mira, the saint from Western India, starting with the phrase "*Mujhechakarrakhoji* (Oh Lord kindly engaged me as your servant)". Sri Ramakrishna Paramahamsa, the latest incarnation of the Hindus, worshipped across the sects, even across the religions and asked his disciples to 'serve human and other beings as forms of God'.

The term '*dasyu*' is also mentioned many times in the Rig-Veda (vide 1.34.7; 1.100.18; 1.51.8; 1.117.21). Etymological meaning of the word '*dasyu*' is, 'one who destroys others'. But this word is used in the Vedic literature in several senses, such as; (1) Superhuman enemies, (2) Human force, (3) Aborigines, (4) Flat nose, ugly and unclean persons, (5) People who do not perform sacrificial rights, (6) People who hategods and are addicted to strange practices. '*Dasyus*' were probably 'native' or primitive settlers of the regions conquered by the Aryans. They might be the 'rebels against the Vedic culture and practices. They were not killed or forcibly converted, but levelled with a derogatory name. In the later Puranic literature the word '*dasyu*' refers to criminals committing atrocities on peace-loving people.

In the contemporary Indian languages, which derive their origin from Sanskrit, the word '*dasyu*' is present. In Bengali, for example, '*dasyu*' now means 'worst type of criminal'. The words '*Daitya*' and '*Dānava*' perhaps meant the criminals from elite origins. According to Purana, '*Daityas*' are the sons of Diti, wife of the famous sage Kashyapa, while *dānavas* are sons of Danu, another wife of Kashyapa.

'*Asura*' is another word found in Hindu scriptures which indicate 'the other'. It is interesting to note that in early Vedic literature (vide Rgveda 1.35.7; 1.131.1) the term denotes the Supreme Spirit. The word is derived from the root'as' ('to exist'), or '*asu*' (*prāṇa* or life-force). So the etymological meaning of the word '*Asura*' is 'self-existent being' or the 'Being of life-force and power'.

Later the meaning changed from 'beneficent god' to 'malevolent spirit or being' in the post-Vedic literature. The Nirukta, the standard Dictionary of Vedic terms, defines 'asuras' as those 'who are not satisfied in their position', 'the ever-fickle' and 'those who are deprived of their positions by the *suras* or *devas*'.

In the epics and *puranasasuras* are depicted as highly ambitious, aggressive, rich, civilized and powerful. But *asuras* are generally self-centred; not caring for common good. Mainly for this trait, they are in conflict with the *suras* or *devas*, who represent the forces of goodness, refinement and sharing. However, great *asura* kings Prahlada, Bali, Sambara and Bāṇa are depicted as devotees of God. *Asuras*, though malevolent beings, were placed above the *Daityas*, and *Danavas* in early scriptures. But gradually, the *asuras* were degraded and identified with daityas and *danavas*, who are devoid of any positive quality except glorious origin.

Rakshasas are 'beings from whom one seeks to protect oneself'. The epics and *Puranas* mention many *rākshasas* or demons. They are generally described as ugly, mis-shaped and with terrible tasks. *Rakshasas* are extremely evil, wicked or malevolent spirits, but we get mention of *Yakshas*, as a type of *rākshasa*, who are good, benevolent and skilful. They are semi-divine and they possess magical powers. In the traditional code of law, *rākshasa-vivaha* is mentioned which is actually equivalent to forcible abduction and rape in its crudest form and is a punishable offence in civilized societies.

'Yavana' is another word mentioned in the Hindu scripture to denote 'the other'. Mahabharata, Vanaparva, (Ch 188) describes '*Yavanas*' as barbarous people. Originally, perhaps the world might have indicated the Ionians or ancient Greeks who invaded India in 4th Century B.C.E. However, Matsyapurana (114.11) considers the country of the *Yavanas* as a part of Bharatvarsa. *Yavanas* are descendants from Turvasu, one of the sons of King Yayati according to Mahabharata (Adiparva 85.34). Ramayana (Balakanda 55) states that the *Yavanas* were produced from the body of the celestial Cow Nandini to fight against the army of Vishwamitra, who was by birth and training a Kshatriya, but later attained Brahman-hood.

'*Mleccha*' is a term used in the 'Satapatha Brahmana (3.2.123 & 24) to mean those who speak an incorrect and corrupt dialect. The non-Aryan people who came from outside India are called *mlecchas* in the epics and *Puranas*. Dharmasutra (9.17) of Gautama prohibits people to live in the company and even speak with *mlecchas*, as they are impure and irreligious people. Perhaps, the people living in the country beyond Aryavarta, where the Varnashrama system was not practiced, were called '*mlecchas*'. Bhavishyapurana (A.D. 900) describes *mlecchas* as eaters of beef and sellers of their own children.

The Mahabharta describes that *mlecchas* were produced from the tail of the celestial Cow Nandini of Vasishtha and drove away the army of Vishwamitra. The story is almost similar to the story about the origin of *Yavanas* as found in the Ramayana. We may infer that the terms '*mleccha*' and '*yavana'* are synonymous. The term '*yavana'* and '*mleccha'* are used in contemporary Bengali literature to refer to invaders belonging to different religions, especially Islam.[8]

---

8 Bankim Chandra Chattopadhyay, who composed '*Vande Mataram'*, the National Hymn, as a part of his novel Anandamath, referred Muslims as *Yavana* in that novel. Both the terms *Yavana* and mulеccha are commonly used in late nineteenth and early twentieth century Bengali Literature.

As noted above, there are several words denoting 'the other' in the scriptures and other books of the Hindus. One such word is '*Para*' which means both 'the other' and 'the Absolute'. Realisation of '*Parabrahma*', i.e, 'the Absolute' is the goal of life. Everything in the universe is included in it, i.e., *Parabrahma*. No one is excluded.

When '*Para*' means 'the other' then also discrimination cannot be the ideal, '*Ayamnija para betiganalaghucetasam, udara caritanam tu vasudhaiva kutumbakam*' (discrimination among people as 'we' and 'they' is done by mean-minded persons only, not liberals). Diversity is not only permissible but desirable also. Diversity makes the world beautiful, lovable and liveable. In fact, Hinduism, as such, is so liberal in outlook that any concept of 'the other' is inconsistent with it. Common people are not sometimes, aware of the liberal principles of Hinduism. They are often guided by local priests, whose survival often depends on spreading conservatism and prejudices.

Hindu society, as a result is both liberal and conservative. Urban elites and non-resident Indians Hindus are very liberal regarding choice of (1) friends and companions, (2) Mates, (3) Food and beverage, (4) Language and many other aspects. But they are conservative about preservation of rituals of ancestors' faith, of course with modification, in response to the demand of time. Rural Hinduism is even now conservative not only regarding 'theother' i.e., the people belonging to other religions, but also regarding the people belonging to castes other than their own. Intensity of caste discrimination is not of same degree all over India. It is almost invisible in Bengal, whereas in Haryana, even nowadays we find honour killing supported by Khat Panchayats in case of love affairs among adult youths of different castes.

It is noteworthy that fundamentalism is inconsistent with Hindu religious tradition, which maintains that all religions are true and can lead its adherents to the ultimate goal, if followed sincerely. Hinduism underwent many changes in course of time. Many undesired rites and rituals are incorporated by the priests and common people are almost convinced that superstitions and unnecessary rituals are part and parcel of Hinduism. To make Hinduism free from such superstition, in the 19th Century, there was a call from Brahmo Samaj to go to the fundamentals of Hinduism, i.e., to the principles as recorded in the Vedas and Upanishads. 'Brahma' was a fundamentalist movement which died its natural death in the 1941 Census, when most of the Brahmas registered their namesas Hindus in response to the clarion call of Rabindranath Tagore, the great litterateur and the first Nobel Laureate in Asia.

Savarkar started another fundamentalist movement to build 'Hindu Nation'. He was a politician, not a person of spiritual realisation. He wanted to capitalise the 'Two Nation' theory to gain power but failed. Independent India adopted secular constitution, but the political leaders wanted to keep people segregated in the name of religion, caste and language, etc. No common criterion for Indian-ness was propagated. Vote Bank Politics was indulged in the name of 'Secularism'. As a reaction, 'majority nationalism' in the name of 'Hindutva' was revived. Hindutva, the brainchild of Savarkar, is out and out political ideology. One should not confuse that with Hinduism, a religious tradition, founded by the seers and saints and rejuvenated by prophets and incarnations. Hindutva, like all other ideologies, is of course exclusivist. However, it wants to include all citizens of India provided they acknowledge India as Holy land, which is nothing but a diplomatic adjustment to avoid conflict.

Political parties, covertly or overtly, make use and misuse the religions sentiments of common people. Administration and judiciary intervene only when that takes the form of violent confrontation. Hypocrisy is rampant and culture of dialogue is almost missing. Conflict is inevitable in any democratic set-up. Culture of patient-hearing and argumentation needs to be developed, one must be liberal enough to recognise human rights of the opponents, even the enemies. Let us pray for well-being of all around us.

'Let everyone be happy, let everybody recover from illness, let everybody say good things alone and let no one suffer.'

7

Follow One [Religion]; Respect All
Maulana Wahiduddin Khan's Pragmatic Approach to Building a Peaceful Community

C. Pursenla Ozukum[1]

Introduction

Maulana Wahiduddin Khan is perhaps one among the most published traditionalist *Sunni* Muslim scholar alive today. He is also one among the leading Muslim thinkers who has developed an understanding of Islam that is appealing to the modern mind while remaining firmly grounded in the authority of the Qur'an and the Hadīth. At a time when Islam is quite easily misunderstood intentionally or naively, Khan presents Islam as a religion of peace. This is evident from his way of equating peace to life and its absence to death. In other words Khan attempts to bridge the gap between traditional Islamic learning and modern knowledge by constructing a bold and versatile interpretation of Islamic textual sources in order to present the concept of peace as a complete ideology.[2] Furthermore, he is one among the *ulema*, who criticizes

1 C. Pursenla Ozukum is a Doctoral Student in Religion under South Asia Theological Research Institute (SATHRI), Senate Serampore College.

2 Irfan Omar, "Towards an Islamic Theology of Nonviolence: A Critical Appraisal of Maulana Wahiduddin Khan's View of Jihad (Part I)" in *Vidyajyoti Journal of Theological Reflection* 72/9, September 2008: 671.

Muslim scholars from within an Islamic framework. This paper is an attempt to bring out Khan's understanding of concepts such as peace and non-violence, and his pragmatic approach towards interfaith relations and building a culture of peace.

Conceptual Formulations: Towards a Theology of Non-Violence

Khan defines non-violence as the active promotion of peace and that should not be confused with inaction or passivity. His understanding of non-violence is quite different to that of Gandhi's approach in which non-violence was a tool that was employed to actively seek justice by way of protest, demonstration and boycott without using physical force. Khan is opposed to public protest, demonstration and mass rallies as a means to strive for peace. Instead he believes in what he calls 'peaceful revolution' whereby each individual takes it up upon him/herself to eradicate violence from within.[3] Khan's 'theology of non-violence' is necessitated by the want to create peaceful co-existence, which is desired for not only the *ahl al-kitāb* or the 'People of the Book,' but to all other peoples and it extends to include all creation.[4] This principle is echoed in celebrated advices offered at many interfaith meeting, 'follow one [religion]; respect all'.

From a pragmatic perspective, Khan is convinced that without peace among various communities, religious or otherwise, humanity as a whole cannot achieve its full potential here on earth. Religious and pragmatic reasons are not separate for Khan, but he presents them separately so as to relate to people at large instead of limiting his message to the Muslims alone. Even as it is necessary for the Muslims to work for peace both in their communal and individual life, it is also required of them by the Qur'an as well as by the demand of conventional wisdom to promote peaceful co-existence with other people within their own community, with people of other faith and the cultures of the world at large.[5]

---

3 Omar, *Towards an Islamic Theology of Nonviolence,* 678-679.

4 Omar, *Towards an Islamic Theology of Nonviolence,* 676.

5 Omar, *Towards an Islamic Theology of Nonviolence,* 676.

In fact, Khan is among one of the few Indian *ulema* to have taken seriously the issue of pluralism and inter-community relations free from stereotyping that generally characterize the response of many Muslims to people of other faith. He writes that every religion upholds certain basic human values, such as a love, compassion, peace and concern for the poor and the marginalized which should form the basis for dialogue initiatives. Therefore, Khan says, Muslims must seek to build bridges with others on the basis of the values that they hold in common. His willingness to appreciate the common values that every religion holds does not however mean that he believes that all religions are equally valid. He insists that Islam is also one among the perfect religions, the reason being that the scripture has survived intact. However, he urges that this consciousness of the truth[6] about Islam should not deter Muslims from being willing to dialogue with others. Hence, this passion for his dialogue is what underlies his approach to issues that relates to peace, jihad and inter-religious/community relations.[7]

Maulana Wahiduddin Khan's Exposition of Peace

Khan writes, "Peace is the only religion for both man and the universe. In a peaceful environment all good things are possible, whereas in the absence of peace, one cannot achieve anything of a positive nature, either as individuals, or as a community."[8] For Khan, peace is not an academic subject rather it's the goal of his existence and his mission of life may be called a 'peace mission'.

---

6 Khan likens the relation between Islam and other religions to that between modern chemistry and ancient alchemy. Comparing Islam to be the modern chemistry which is based on 'facts proved', while the other religion as the ancient alchemy which are grounded in 'unproven speculations.' Therefore, for those who are seeking the truth the difference is so evident that Islam will be the only choice as it's the only religion having historical credibility. [Maulana Wahiduddin Khan, *Islam Rediscovered: Discovering Islam from its Original Source* (New Delhi: Goodword Books, 2010), 45].

7 Khan, *Jihad, Peace and Inter-community Relations in Islam*, xvi-xxi.

8 Maulana Wahiduddin Khan, *A Manifesto of Peace* (New Delhi: Goodword Books, 2001), 5.

He is a born pacifist but Khan notes that his pacifism is not a strategic nature. Rather it is a formula for justifying support in one case or opposition in another. His pacifism extends to all of humanity and bears a positive value in the full sense of the word. It is the absolute good and not a theory.[9] In his opinion, peace is not a developed discipline although there is this term 'pacifism', which according to him is the study of other aspect of peace. There are departments under peace, but not as a developed subject as it is not easy to discover the laws of peace. He further outlines that it may be a general tendency among scholars to discover the laws that entwine a particular discipline but in peace it is not possible to discover them because wo(man) is not predictable and cannot impose a peaceful discipline on him/her. Peace is rather a voluntary behavior, and cannot be imposed as a 'discipline' on anyone. So, pacifism is the alternative which according to Khan can be termed as a discipline though not well developed in its full sense.[10]

Though scholars in general define peace as 'the absence of war', Khan says one cannot impose a negative connotation on defining the term 'Peace' because it has a positive value which is 'the highest good'. He defines 'Peace' to be the presence of opportunities and opening the door to opportunities.[11] Unlike other scholars who hold the position that peace devoid of justice is no peace, Khan does not link peace with justice because peace on its own does not bring justice. That is, justice is not necessarily an element of peace.

Khan so well asserts that violence and peace both have wide connotations. Violence includes everything from hatred to war so is peace from tolerance to love. He opines that it is due to the lack

---

9 Maulana Wahiddundin Khan, *The Ideology of Peace: Towards a Culture of Peace* (New Delhi: Goodword Books, 2010), 8.

10 *Interview* with Maulana Wahiduddin Khan, New Delhi, 21st April 2012.

11 According to Khan, peace will give the opportunity and by availing to it Justice can be obtained. It creates favorable conditions that would enable one to strive for justice and other constructive ends. Peace is always desirable for its own sake. Everything else comes after peace, not along with peace.

of wisdom and ideology that people generally do not know the value of peace - which is the complete code of conduct. Peace, according to him, means normalcy and normalcy provides all such opportunities that favor the growth of a healthy environment, it fosters the highest level of human culture. He quotes one of Jesus Christ's greatest teaching "Love your enemies" and interprets in his own language that 'one should live peacefully with his enemies' i.e., to win over one's enemy by using the power of peace.[12]

Islam as a Religion of Peace according to Khan

Islam is a religion of peace in the fullest sense of the word as the Quran justifies its way 'the path of peace' (*Sūrah Al-Mā'idah*, 5:16).[13] Seldom is this core universal truth of their religion misunderstood by their followers.

Khan makes this strong affirmation that Islam and violence are contradictory to each other and that Islamic terrorism is a contradiction in terms, much as 'pacifist' terrorism. He holds firmly that the teachings of Islam are based directly or indirectly on the principles of peace. In his interpretation, 'Islam' connotes peace. According to Khan, the position of peace in Islam is a

12 *Interview* with Maulana Wahiduddin Khan.

13 Maulana Wahiduddin Khan, *Islam Rediscovered: Discovering Islam from its Original Sources* (New Delhi: Goodword Books, 2010), 91.

value, while war in Islam is allowed only in exceptional[14] cases when it cannot be avoided.[15]

Khan's works in their entirety are also concerned with the interpretation of Islam as a 'peaceful religion'. He opines, harmony begins with the understanding of the self and the self's role in the universe as enjoined by the divine commandments in the Quran which eventually leads to the establishment of peace (*salām*), both inner and outer.[16] He insists that Islam as a religion in itself is the foundation for spiritual, religious, social and universal peace. His ultimate interest in peace as reflected in his works and practice finds its basis in the religion of Islam itself. Therefore, he sets out his education of Islam centered on the principle of peace - "Islam is the answer to the demands of nature"[17] says Khan. It is the goal of Islam to counter human failings and to attempt to maintain a natural course of the human journey towards the Creator. Human nature desires 'peace and love' which are also the demands of Islam.[18]

---

14 Refer commentary of *Sūrah al-Baqarah,* 2:190. Here, Khan also brings into light the Christian scripture (Mathew 10:34: Do not think that I came to bring Peace on Earth. I did not come to bring peace, but a sword) conjoining that it would not be right to even conclude that the religion preached by Christ was one of war and violence, for such utterances relate purely to particular occasions. So far as general life is concerned, Christ taught peaceful values, such as the building up of good character, loving each other, helping the poor and needy, etc. And also for instance, the *Gita*, the Holy book of the Hindus, pertains to wisdom and moral values. Yet along with this is the exhortation of Krishna to Arjun, encouraging him to fight (3:30). So according to Khan, this does not mean that believers in the Gita should wage wars all the time. Gandhi after all derived his non-violence from the same *Gita*. [See: Maulana Wahiduddin Khan, *The True Jihad: The Concept of Peace, Tolerance and Non-Violence in Islam, 43-44]*

15 Maulana Wahiduddin Khan, *The True Jihad: The Concept of Peace, Tolerance and Non-Violence in Islam* (New Delhi: Goodword Books, 2002), 30.

16 Omar, *Towards an Islamic Theology of Nonviolence*: 675-676.

17 As quoted in Omar, *Towards an Islamic Theology of Non-Violence-I*, 676.

18 Omar, *Towards an Islamic Theology of Non-Violence-I*, 676-677.

The line where he differs in the interpretation of Islam as a religion of Peace is his connectivity with the spiritual aspect of human relation to God and nature where God becomes the center from whom peace prevails. He conjures that;

> "Peace is a universal law of nature. That is because God loves the condition of peace and disproves of any state of unrest. God's predilection for peace is quite enough reason for the believer also to love peace. In no circumstances will the true believer ever tolerate the disruption of peace."[19]

Therefore, his attestation of peace to one of the attributes of God which is described in the Quran as *As-Salam* becomes the basis for his thesis on Islam as a religion of peace. *As-Salam* means peace and security, well-being, integrity, etc., that is to say that God's being itself is a manifestation of *peace*. Indeed, 'God is peace' (*Al-Bukhari*)/Khan further delineates that in the Quran, divine guidance is likened to the paths of peace. Further averting that 'reconciliation is best' (*Sūrah An-Nisā'*, 4:128), and judging by the consequences, the way of peace is far better than that of confrontation.[20] The Quran declares that no aggressive war is permitted in Islam for ". . . *Allah loves not the aggressors. . .*[21] *whereby Allah guides such as to follow His pleasure into ways of peace and brings them out of darkness into light by His will and guides them to the right path.*"[22] One can also note that the Prophet Muhammad so earnestly used to entreat his Lord in his daily prayers; O God, You are the original source of Peace; from You is all Peace, and to You returns all Peace. So, make us live with Peace; and let us enter paradise, the House of Peace. Blessed be You, our Lord, to whom belongs all Majesty and Honour![23]

---

19 Maulana Wahiduddin Khan, *Principles of Islam* (New Delhi: Goodword Books, 2010), 100.

20 Khan, *The True Jihad,* 30-31.

21 Ali, *The Holy Qur'an*, 80.

22 *Sūrah al-Māidah, 5:16* in Ali, *The Holy Qur'an*, 246.

23 Maulana Wahidudding Khan, "Solution to Terrorism" http://cpsglobal.org/content/solutio-terrorism. Accessed on 3rd May 2012.

According to Islam, in the view of Khan, paradise is the ideal human abode and is thus called the 'Home of Peace' where people of paradise will wish peace to one another indicating the social culture of people of paradise will be based on peace.[24] Therefore, with this vision, Khan sets out to envision a 'culture of peace' and propose it as a remedial for a terror-stricken context and also to propagate the true message of Islam which in entirety according to Khan is Peace and calls the people of other faith to judge Islam in the light of its teachings and not otherwise.

Religion of Islam Censures Violence

Khan says there is no basis of violence in Islam. It is wholly a religion of peace and humanism. The very first verse of the *Quran*; *Bismillahiar-Rahmaniar-Rahim* (In the name of *Allah*, the most Merciful, the most compassionate) repeated no less than 114 times shows the great importance that Islam attaches to values such as mercy and compassion.[25] There is also a verse in the Quran which reads: *And God calls to the home of peace*[26] implying that the destination of Islam is peace. All the teachings are oriented towards the goal of peace. The *Quran* too presents the universe as a model of peace; *neither is it for the sun to overtake the moon, nor can the night outstrip the day. And all float on in one orbit.*[27] Holding up this phenomenon as an ideal, Khan says, the *Quran* too models to follow the same course of peace, that is, to move in one's own orbit and not trespass. Thus peaceful living is the religion for both human and the universe.[28]

Khan cites another tradition of the Prophet which reads; "*Don't wish for confrontation with your enemy, instead always ask for peace from Allah", a*nd interprets that even when they have enemies, Muslims are not encouraged to take course of

24 Khan, *The True Jihad,* 31.

25 Khan, *Islam Rediscovered,* 91.

26 *Sūrah Yūnus*, 10:25 in Ali, *The Holy Qur'an*, 423. *Cf.*, Khan, *Islam as Peace.*

27 *Sūrah YāSīn*, 36:40 in Ali, *The Holy Qur'an*, 846. *Cf.*, Khan, *Islam as Peace*

28 Khan, *Islam as Peace.*

confrontation rather seek the way of avoidance. Also citing a verse from the Quran, "*that if you deal with your enemy positively and return good for evil, he will become your closest friend.*"[29] In the same light, Khan addresses the misconception of *jihad* attested to Islam as a religion of violence using the word. According to Khan, *jihad* means a struggle, a peaceful struggle to be performed by the power of ideology rather than the power of the sword; it is only another name for peaceful activism along Islamic lines.[30] He quotes from the *Quran,* "strive for the cause of *Allah* as it behooves you to strive for it". (*Sūrah al-Hajj*, 22: 78)[31]

At the turn of this century, Khan contends, there is a great need that Islam be studied from its original scriptures in order to re-discover it in its original form as non-Muslims have mistakenly come to regard Islam as a religion of intolerance and violence. Without a doubt, the problem of misapprehension applies exclusively to Islam. Khan has been at this point been critical when he addresses why there should ever have a misapprehension about Islam and its adherence. The reasons, he opines, are not based on any allegation but rather on the fact that the Muslims today in almost every country display violence and intolerance towards others. With no suspicion, one can say that the Muslims adopted this course of action in the name of Islamic movements or Islamic Jihad. The erroneous conception also runs through in [their] understanding of the Prophet of Islam as they later glorified him as a national hero, so that Muslims might assert their own superiority over the other nations.[32]

The other reason attested for misapprehension about Islam according to Khan is the educated masses of the modern times obsessed with the concept of anthropology, which treats religion as a social phenomenon instead as a vehicle for revealed truth.

---

29 *Sūrah Fussilat*, 41:34 in Ali, *The Holy Qur'an*, 911. *Cf.*, Khan, *Islam as Peace.*

30 Khan, *Islam as Peace.*

31 Khan, *The True Jihad,* 13.

32 Maulana Wahiduddin Khan, "Islam as Peace" http://cpsglopal.org/fag-view. Accessed on 3rd May 2012.

Therefore, it further regards the activities of Muslims to be Islam and that the activities that Muslims are engaged in are in the name of Islam.[33] Khan, analyzing all the aspects calls for a creation of an entirely new Muslim leadership and community, one that seeks to lead the community to a path of construction rather than one of confrontation. Khan's activism is not just for people who are not Muslims but also for the whole Muslim community. Therefore, peace and building bridges with people of other faiths on the basis of the values they hold in common, then, becomes a matter of particular urgency for Muslims. If that were to happen, he suggests to convince others that the Islamic faith can offer viable solutions to many problems and apprehensions affecting the society.[34]

Intolerance versus Mutual Respect

Classical Islamic law divides the citizens of *dar al-harb* (house/abode of war) into two groups; *ahl al-kitab* (People of the book-Jew, Christian, Sabi'in) and *Mushrikum* (Polytheist). They live comfortably under Islamic rule as long as they fulfill their duties (*ahlal-dhimmi*) that they pay the *jizya.*[35] According to the Islamic law, Muslims should offer two choices to *Mushrikum; either* converting to Islam or death. Yet, this action was rarely taken after the Muslims conquest Arabia. Muslims usually treated all non-Muslims in the same manner as the *ahl al-kitab.* After the Muslim's conquest of India, the concept of *ahl al-kitab* eventually extended to Hindus as well. These historical facts eventually suggest that 'conversion or death' approach in propagation was not adopted by Muslims and terminology such as *Mushrikum* became obsolete among Muslims.[36] This shows that Islam teaches

33 Khan, *Islam as Peace.*

34 Khan, *Jihad, Peace and Inter-Community Relations in Islam*, xviii-xx.

35 *Jizyah* is a special tax required to be paid by non-Muslim in lieu of protection and exemption from military service. However, objective Scholars understands that non-Muslims living in an Islamic state were offered complete protection against foreign armies despite not having to serve in the military. If any non-Muslim served in the army, the *jizyah* was not levied. [See: Saiyad Fareed Ahmad, *How Can We Understand Diversity:* 18]

36 Baidhawy, *The Concept of Jihad and Mujahid Peace*, 43.

tolerance and mutual respect. Islam not only refrains from showing disrespect to their religious authorities but also recognizes and respects prophets of all religions, both known and unknown. (3:84).[37] Khan identifies the exchange of views on religious issues that took place between the three monotheistic religions namely Islam, Christianity and Judaism at Medina – a trialogue,[38] as the first inter-faith exchange.

Khan's Approach towards Interfaith Relations

Dialogue as the Way to Peace

Khan considers dialogue as the way to peace toward which he has made great roads in establishing conversations between Muslims and Hindus and even Christians on a host of issues. In his effort to win over the Hindu right-wing groups, he has participated in their meeting to show what he calls 'true' Islam- an Islam which does not 'otherize' or seek to alienate and an Islam which calls for peace not reprisal and retaliation. To some certain extent these efforts to bring the extremists among Hindus closer to accepting Muslims as fellow Indians (they were otherwise viewed as 'foreigners') have been productive.[39] According to him, constructing divisions between 'us' and 'them' are opposed by the *Quran's methods*, which instead encourages one to exchange dialogues between different groups.[40] Khan has won respect among many such Hindus maintaining an interesting 'alliance.' In Khan's view, it is imperative that Muslims seek direct talks with Hindu neighbors and try to build bridges with them instead of creating an environment of hostility by regarding them as the 'other'. Khan believes that Muslims should try harder to resolve their differences directly with their Hindu neighbors or 'the other'. Thus, dialogue can benefit all communities by facilitating cooperation on common issues across the broad, but such dialogue is also open to missionary activity.

37 Abdul Ali, *Ethical Framework of Islam for Peaceful Co-existence*, 75.

38 Khan, *Islam as Peace.*

39 Omar, *Islamic Thought in Contemporary India,* 80.

40 Omar, *Islam and the Other,* 431.

Hence, all communities would have the right to 'present' their religious teachings to others without engaging in proselytizing.[41]

The Role of Islam in Promoting a 'Culture of Peace' in Khan's thought

There has been a great contradiction between the principles of Islam and the practices of Muslims. Khan identifies one root cause as to be traced to the historical exigency as the compilation of Islamic history has tended to read like an uninterrupted series of wars and conquests.[42] The stress lies on the fact that Prophet Muhammad was upheld by the Muslims as a national hero which on many occasions has been misrepresented by historians as a military leader. Therefore, basing on the allegation of Khan that Islam is based on the principle of peace and that Prophet Muhammad adhered strictly to peaceful means, he moves forward with how Islam be made relevant in a culture progressing towards peace.

One modern form of transgression as forbidden in the *Quran* which says, "Do not transgress the bounds of your religion"[43] is what is now called the Islamic Fundamentalism or Islamic Extremism. Since, the *Quran* is imbued with the spirit of peace and tolerance, its culture is not that of war but of mercy.[44] And from then, Islam should begin to fill the ideological vacuum created in disassociating themselves from the main stream.

Khan critiques that in modern time, the violent approach of the intellectuals and leaders of the *ummah* (Muslim community) or of the movement(s) are responsible for the violent mentality among Muslims. This mentality has alienated them from their neighbors. The only way, according to Khan, is to alleviate the tragic plight of Muslims back to non-violent Islam ranging

41 Omar, *Islamic Thought in Contemporary India,* 80-81.

42 Maulana Wahiduddin Khan, *Islamic Fundamentalism* (New Delhi: Goodword Books, 2003), 10.

43 *Surah Al-Nisā'*, 4:17 *The Quran* translated by Maulana Wahiduddin Khan, edited by Farida Khanam (New Delhi: Goodword Books, 2009),58.

44 Khan, *Islamic Fundamentalism*, 6-8.

from the social to education and extending it to equality of their partnership with the rest of the world's community.[45]

One injunction that the Muslim Fundamentalist holds about Islam, according to Khan, is to build an ideal society, an ideal state and then launch a violent movement. Though 'ideal state' and 'ideal society' has a prime resonance, according to Khan, the terms are misused and are a sheer exploitation of Islam. There are injunctions in the *Quran* and *Hadith* that the Muslims are enjoined to establish an ideal state and that idealism and perfection are highly desirable virtues in Islam. Therefore, Khan ratifies that the Islamic idealism is not society and of the state but the individual. Its perennial objective being to make individual an ideal human being an example of 'sublime character' projected by the Prophet Muhammad.[46] The reason that Khan makes it important to refer to the *Quran* and *Hadith* and draw examples from Prophet Muhammad is because Muslims today have deviated from the main teachings and principles of Islam and does not follow the *sunnah* of the Prophet.

Down the centuries revivalist has attempted renewal (*tajdīd*) of Islam that would best suit the modern mind and milieu. He strongly asserts that it is the Muslims who have forgotten how to reinterpret and reapply Islam in accordance to the needs and circumstances of the times. He argues that what is impaired in the Indian Muslims community (in particular) is a coherent and articulate vision of the reapplication of the Islamic ideals. These ideals in Khan's exposition are pluralism, tolerance of differences, utilizing peaceful means to activism and becoming progressive within the scope of the teachings of Islam.[47] This is what the *Quran* teaches, the *Sunnah* explicates and what the Prophet of Islam accomplished.

The ambivalent attitude that Khan observes among the present day Muslims is that they tend to endorse violence as an instrument for self defense and the obligation of religious norms.

---

45 Khan, *The True Jihad,* 92-93.

46 Khan, *Islamic Fundamentalism*, 15-16.

47 Omar, *Islamic Thought in Contemporary India*, 85.

Generally, people understand religion as supporting non violence on one hand and advocates intolerance and violence on the other. One can also observe that just a position of religion Islam can be the bearer of peace and of the sword. Thus, Khan's assertion is that there is a need to reinterpret religion and its teaching so that they are without ambiguity, misconception and manipulation. Khan affirms that true religion speaks not of war but urges the promise of peace, love, justice and oneness which is wholly reflected in the pages of the Quran and in the life of Prophet Muhammad.[48]

Therefore, Khan feels that if Muslims begin to apply the reinterpretation of Islam, best appealing to the present context, it will exhilarate and restore the willingness of each faith order or religions to collaborate in maintaining a multi-cultural ethos and extend to the culture where peace would prevail.[49] This he feels would be the *kairos*, an opportune time for Muslims to present the true face of Islam and the extensiveness of their tolerance.

Daw'ah Activism

Daw'ah is in fact another name for peaceful struggle for the propagation of Islam. Therefore, *daw'ah* activism is in fact Islamic activism.[50] According to Khan, Islam is based on this principle of *daw'ah,* which in an inter-religious context may also be understood as a method of peaceful negotiation through which Khan advertently projects Islam as a non-violent religion.

Khan argues that the Muslim community is still atrophied in memories of their glorious past[51] and further explains that it is the Muslims' religious and secular leaders who are actually responsible for the violent approach on the part of Muslim today.[52] Therefore, it is quite apparent that he refrains from blaming

48 Interview with Maulana Wahiduddin Khan.

49 Omar, *Islamic Thought in Contemporary India*, 85.

50 Maulana Wahiduddin Khan, *Non-Violence in Islam* (New Delhi: Goodword Books, 2003), 37.

51 Irfan A. Omar, "Indian Muslims and the Search for Communal Harmony: Some Notes on Maulana Wahiduddin Khan" in *Studies in Contemporary Islam* 2/1, 2000: 64.

52 Khan, *Non-Violence in Islam,* 40.

external factors for the communal conflicts, holding none but Muslims responsible for the conflicts.[53]

Khan sees that the violent mentality of the Muslims is responsible for having alienated them from their neighbors everywhere. This clearly shows that they no longer esteem the ideal of universal brotherhood/sisterhood and they are looked upon with aversion and dread. This dissociation has left Muslims a backward group in modern times and therefore has neglected opportunities for *daw'ah*. Khan discerns for the need to alleviate the tragic plight of Muslims to bring them back to the non-violent version of Islam.[54] Therefore, Khan with the principle of *daw'ah* activism not only tries to bring Islam to the path of non-violence and revive Islam but also tries to projects the true face of Islam.

In the recent past, Khan's model of peaceful interaction - *daw'ah* activism has also helped the Muslims stimulate intellectually as interactions facilitated the task of *daw'ah* dynamically. It was from the point view of *daw'ah* that peaceful interactions and dialogue between Muslims and the so-called non-Muslims have stabilized.[55] At the same time, there is also a shift in the style of thinking of many people from violent activism to peaceful activism and that more people are convinced of peaceful means for the defense of Islam and Muslim.[56]

The key objective for the movement in fact was a call to the Muslims to engage in *ijtihād* and rethink and articulate a new core message of Islam in light of modern challenges and its applications. His concern also delves to the extent of educating the *Imams* not only Islamically but also on other matters as they become the most influential point of reference for all the Muslims. They needed to be well-versed with the *sharī'ah* and Islamic theology as they play a very significant role.[57] By this, Khan hopes that Muslims

---

53 Omar, *Indian Muslims and the Search for Communal Harmony,* 65.

54 Khan, *Non-Violence in Islam,* 41-42.

55 Khan, *Non-Violence in Islam,* 42-43.

56 Khan, *Islam and Peace*, translated by Dr. Farida Khanam (New Delhi: Goodword Books, 2008), 233.

57 Khan, *Blasphemy in Islam.*

can rewrite the history of Islam provided they make timely use of opportunities as it is only the Muslims themselves who can show the rest of the world that Islam is a religion of peace.[58] These amounts to a reform from within; the key components of this rethinking are nonviolence and reconciliation.[59]

Conclusion

Maulana Wahiduddin Khan invites to an understanding of pluralism while remaining faithful to one's own tradition. It is true that every religion possess religious models as mobilizing resources to come to a common table of concern. According to Khan it is peace, dialogue, respect and understanding lying at the core of every religion. His rationale to this end is for a peaceful co-existence with other communities therefore, he fights the differences that exist because living side by side with the 'other' is an everyday encounter. Since a commitment to the praxis of inter-religious understanding has become the urgent need of the present times, Khan's understanding of non-violence, tolerance and peace process towards interfaith relations remains aloof from politics and inclines towards human morality and spirituality. The reason is politics being manifest in the form of corruptions, violence, conflicts and injustice that contrast the culture of peace that he envisions. With all these delineations it is apparent that Khan has tried to present Islam, taking into account the religio-cultural ethos, as a religion that contrives for peace holding importance to moral and spiritual values. It is at this crux that Khan befittingly couples human spirituality which will lead to a progressive process of peace and moves to wider realm of the common human 'culture of peace.'

Today the question of global peace associates not only with religion but also concerns the socio-economic, socio-political and religio-cultural stability and all these contextual elements - cultural fundamentals, undeniability of human essentials conditions human morality. As Khan rightly points, the basic of

58 Khan, *The True Jihad,* 71-95.

59 Omar, *Islamic Thought in Contemporary India*, 79.

all religion is the wellbeing of all human kind in the society and their dignity. It is religion which pulls them together and gives them the basic instinct of co-existence and uses its competency in achieving peace. Hence, when one talks about peace, it is not just the theoretical orientation but a pragmatical progress associates the principle that surrounds 'peace.'

Khan's susceptibility to the necessities of the context groaning with socio-religious conflicts and violence is very much prominent through the commitment towards building a common human culture of peace. It is infact creditable of Khan's attempt to engage himself with the mainstream non-Muslim and seriously taking the inter-community relationship and plurality fostering a polemic free community.

8

Guthi: Institutions for Facilitating Interfaith Interactions

Dhanbir Rai[1]

Introduction

During my numerous field trips[2] to the three city states of Kathmandu, Bhaktapur and Patan from 2010-2013, I would wander around the long stretches of buildings that seem to be endless. These closely knitted buildings belong to the *Newars*[3]

---

1 Rev. Dr. Dhanbir Rai teaches Religion and the Dean of Post Graduate Studies at Clark Theological College, Mokokchung, Nagaland.

2 I made series of trips to Kathmandu, Bhaktapur and Patanfrom 2010 – 2013 for my research among the *newars*.

3 Traditionally, the *newars* are considered as the indigenous inhabitants of the Kathmandu valley. Today, the term 'Newar' embraces people of both Mongoloid and Mediterranean physical types who speak both Nepali and *Newari* that includes some half a dozen dialects. The *newars* are divided into two main religious groups. They are *Bauddhamargis*, worshippers of *Buddha* and *Sivamargis*, worshippers of *Siva*. Cf. Bimal Shrestha, *Social Life in Nepal* (Biratnagar: Vani Prakashan Co-operative Ltd., 1997); David N. Gellner, "Introduction" in *Contested Hierarchies: A Collaborative Ethnography of Caste among the Newars of Kathmandu Valley, Nepal,* 2nd Impression (New Delhi: Oxford University Press, 2003); Dor Bahadur Bista, *People of Nepal*, 7th edition (Kathmandu: Ratna Pustak Bhandar, 2000); Gopal Singh Nepali, *The Newars: An Ethno-Sociological Study of a*

who have double headed caste hierarchy.[4] These connected buildings seem to tell me that there is healthy interfaith and moral order maintained by the *newars* in spite of religious and caste distinction and hierarchy. I started to question how *newars* belonging to different religions and castes co-existed side by side that was separated by a narrow alley. Living in close proximity one cannot avoid interaction day in and day out which is incongruous in a religious and caste based society. An elderly *newar* who resided in one of the cramped buildings candidly remarked, "hamimilerajhulerabasincha" which can be translated as "we live joyfully and in unity". This led me to regard the *newar* spirituality of living together as human beings in high esteem. Their assurance of peaceful and community living led me deeper into the study of *newar* religions and culture, particularly interfaith interactions. In the process, I stumbled over the practice of *guthi*[5] by the *newars*.

Consideration of Common Utterances

The phrase "*hamimilerajhulerabasincha*" goes a long way in interfaith interactions among the *newars*. It signifies religious tolerance, respect, equality, honesty, loyalty and being in the same

---

Himalayan Community (Kathmandu: Himalayan Booksellers, 1988 Reprint 1965).

4 The *newars* are divided hierarchically into castes, from *Brahman* to "untouchables", and consist of more than 30 main caste groups. Caste is the principle basis of social hierarchy for both the hindu and the Buddhist *newars*. In theory the *newar* caste organization is based on the same Hindu principle which stipulates the five-fold division of society: the *Brahmin*, the *Kshatriya*, the *Vaisya*, the *Sudra* and the "untouchable." The *newar* buddhists and the Hindus have coexisted and interacted with each other and complicated further the whole framework of the *newar* structure. This double headed caste structure is unique to the *newars* and with contradictory internal tensions in the hierarchy set up. Gerard Toffin, *Newar Society: City, Village and Periphery,* 2nd edition (Lalitpur: Himal Books, 2008).

5 *Guthis* are uniquely *newar* institutions, which control most aspects of their social and religious life, including the multitude of family and calendrical festivals which dominate social life. John Mellowship, *The Enchanted World of Kumari* (Varanasi: Pilgrims Publishing, 2007), p. 27.

rhythmic moral order of life. To the *newars*, each individual, irrespective of religious differences, has the same importance like that of the other and requires equal respect and recognition. Their community assures of human dignity which demands same reciprocation in their religious, social and cultural interactions. This would mean establishing justice within their complex caste divisions. Is the phrase "hamimilerajhulerabasincha" simply to display interfaith harmony in superficial level of their public discourse? Perhaps, their public discourse can be genuine utterances of negating religious intolerance and caste hierarchy among the *newars*. During my discourse with Karmacharya[6] I was told, "hamisabaidajubhaihun" (we all are brothers). Perhaps, this was to mean acceptance of other faith traditions and mutual recognition among the various caste groups. This phrase was exemplified when he invited me, a Nepali brother from another faith, for dinner. As a priest, he could transcend religious, ritual, social and cultural boundaries and exhibited religious and moral equality through this significant gesture. His genuine cultural and religious engagement culminated in accepting others as 'dajubhai' in its truest sense. Does it mean that the religious differences and caste hierarchy disappears in *newar* spiritual space?

Caste Hierarchy

Solidarity of the *newars* has often led other Nepalese to consider them as a community fused into a common social tradition.[7] But, it would be an over estimation to consider them as a single social group. Scholars like Toffin opine that the *newars* are divided by caste, religion, locality, and dialect makes the question of *newar* ethnicity a highly complex one.[8]

---

6 *Interview* with Udhav Man Karmacharya, Chief Priest, Taleju Temple in Durbar Square, Kathmandu, 04 September 2010.

7 Gopal Singh Nepali, *The Newars: An Ethno-Sociological Study of a Himalayan Community,* op. cit., p. 18.

8 David N. Gellner, "Introduction" in *Contested Hierarchies: A Collaborative Ethnography of Caste Among the Newars of Kathmandu Valley, Nepal,* op.cit., p. 4.

Toffin[9] documented a complex caste hierarchy which is a challenge to equality among the Buddhist and Hindu *newars*. Various ethnographers have presented one sided conceptual social hierarchy of *newars* which undermine the way *newars* have expressed their religious and moral ideology. The phrase "hamisabaidajubhaihun" is in direct contrast to the religious dichotomy and caste hierarchy practiced by the *newars*. As they interact with various religious and caste members in *mandap*,[10] *sattal* or *pati*,[11] the ideology of religious bigotry and caste hierarchy is often questioned. The idea of equality, brotherhood, humanhood is thinly separated with that of religious and caste hierarchy in their moral and public interactions. Many *newars* have shown religious and moral equivalence by practicing brotherhood, mutual sharing, respect and thereby negating the religious and caste hierarchy.

The *newar* caste system is divided into two major divisions. The first division is between the hindu and the buddhist castes. The second division is between pure and impure castes. This gradation was done while dealing with the ethnographic descriptions of the various castes.[12] Many *newars* consider the hierarchy of pure and impure in context of relative moral considerations. Thus, they seek multiple affiliations to various *phukis*[13] and *guthis*[14] which give them alternative hierarchies to establish themselves as human beings and can affirm "hamisabaidajubhaihun". Further, ideas of

---

9 He pioneered in documenting the social structure of the *newar* squite elaborately.

10 Resting place in public places where people of various rest and interact.

11 *Sattal* and *Pati* are the resting places for the travelers. In *sattal*, travelers can stay overnight whereas in *pati*, travelers rest for some moments only.

12 Gopal Singh Nepali, *The Newars: An Ethno-Sociological Study of a Himalayan Community,* op. cit., p. 149.

13 *Phuki* is a term that may be used to describe a link to a common male ancestor. Gerard Toffin, *Newar Society: City, Village and Periphery,* op. cit., pp. 28-30.

14 David N. Gellner, *Monk, Householder, and Tantric Priest: Newar Buddhism and its Hierarchy of Ritual* (New Delhi: Cambridge University Press India Pvt. Ltd, reprint 2009), p. 91.

moral discourses that oppose caste hierarchy are discussed further in their cultural and religious institutions.

Guthi Institutions

Guthis[15] are unique *newar* institutions that exhibit solidarity, brotherhood, sharing, equality, respect, loyalty and honesty. *Newars* participate in two or multiple *guthis* that govern their religious and moral life which has far reaching effect in Kathmandu city. *Guthis* allow the *newars* to relate with one another as they affiliate to *guthis* that can be religious, social and of public service. *Guthisansthan* (institution) oversees the operation of socio-cultural lifestyle of the *newars*. *Guthi* institutions bind the *newars* together at the three different levels of caste, patrilineal grouping and territory. Each provides numerous occasions for collective worship of a particular deity to which it is consecrated; and for feasts in which its members have the right to ritual participation.[16] There are numerous *guthi* institutions that grant scholarships to the individual house-hold groups. These groups divide the *newars* horizontally in a number of groups for achieving different objectives.[17] Of these, the caste *guthis* and the *phukiguthis*[18] are most effective in context of group control. The *dewaliguthi*,[19] the

---

15 The term 'guthi' is derived from the Sanskrit *gosthi*, meaning an 'assembly' or 'society.' *Guthis* are uniquely *newar* institutions, which control most aspects of their social and religious life. The history of *guthi* is as old as the history of *newar* civilization, however, the mentioning of the term dates back to 464 AD, in the inscription found in *Changu Narayan* Temple of Bhaktapur, which is regarded as the first written evidence of Nepalese history. Gopal Singh Nepali, "The Newars" in *An Analysis of Nepali Culture and Society*, edited by Bishnu Prasad Dahal (Lalitpur: Adhikari Books and Stationary, 2004), p. 24.

16 Gopal Singh Nepali, *The Newars: An Ethno-Sociological Study of a Himalayan Community*, op.cit., p. 191.

17 Gopal Singh Nepali, *The Newars: An Ethno-Sociological Study of a Himalayan Community*, op.cit., p. 420.

18 A term applied to the agnatic members coming under a common *Dewali Guthi*.

19 An institution that perpetuates the cult of ancestors through feasts and festivals of the *Dewali* deity, *Dewali Guthi* is also known as *Deo-Guthi*.

main *phukiguthi*, is the real means of upholding the norms of the society through rituals, values and ideas. This feature speaks for the well-knit functioning of the patrilineal solidarity within the frame-work of religion and caste. The entire net-work of social relations in the *newar* community is kept strong through the feasts and festivals under the auspices of the various *guthis*. It is through the participation in these feasts that a *newar* individual enjoys the protection of the society.[20]

Religious type of *guthi* is best explained through the multi-caste cult of tutelary deities which is organized by *newars* belonging to various castes that play a crucial role in Nepali society.[21] The *Kumariguthi* is represented by around 12 of the *newar* castes, such as *Maharjan, Khadgi, Karmacharya, Rajopadya*, and even some *Parbatiyas*.[22] Here, tantric and brahmanic priests, astrologers, storekeepers, farmers, gardeners, butchers, washer-men, musicians, fishermen and sweepers participate.[23] Religious *guthis* were maintained and given unbroken continuity through the *guthisansthan* or land endowments.[24] Mutual recognition of each individual is crucial in sustaining multi-caste *guthi* where their affirmation of community is expressed silently but through ritual participation.

Social interaction is visible through the institution of *sanaguthi*[25] that incorporates religious,[26] service-oriented, communal as well as entertainment-oriented features. It is religious in the sense that it takes divinity to public domain where divine

---

20 Gopal Singh Nepali, *The Newars: An Ethno-Sociological Study of a Himalayan Community,* op. cit., p. 420.

21 Anne Vergati, *Gods, Men and Territory: Society and Culture in Kathmandu Valley*, 1995, Reprint (New Delhi: Manohar Publishers and Distributors, 2002), pp. 106-110.

22 Gerard Toffin, *Newar Society: City, Village and Periphery,* op. cit., p. 294.

23 Gerard Toffin, *Newar Society: City, Village and Periphery,* op. cit., p. 294.

24 Bimala Shrestha, *Social Life in Nepal* (Biratnagar: Vani Prakashan Co-operative Ltd., 1997), p. 18.

25 One of the most commonly practiced *guthi*among the *newars.*

26 Here, *Dyahor or Deo Pyakha*- dances of various Hindu gods and goddesses, are displayed in the streets of *newar* localities.

dancers descend into human domain.[27] It is service-oriented as it incorporates *si guthi or sonam guthi* that performs mortuary rites[28] which is based on caste or sub-caste and locality.[29] The main task of the *siguthi* is to arrange the funeral[30] procession and assist the bereaved household in cremating the deceased person.[31] The ritual of the *siguthi* helps the members to strengthen social ties and establish group solidarity.[32] Social *guthis* organize entertainment, fellowship and activities of common interest.[33]

---

27 Dhanbir Rai, "Pyakhas: Art of the Divine in a mundane world" in *Journal of Tribal Studies*, (Vol. XIX, No. 2, July-December, 2014), pp. 1-23.

28 Ajaya Kranti Shakya, *The Shakyas* (Kathmandu: Nepal Buddhist Development and Research Centre, 2006), p. 157.

29 Each mortuary rites association consists of members from the same caste that live in a particular locality, of a village, town or city. Rajendra PD. Pradhan, "Domestic and Cosmic Rituals among the Hindu Newars of Kathmandu, Nepal" (Ph. D. dissertation, University of Delhi, 1986), p. 40.

30 Every year during the annual worship of *siguthi* deity, a number of households are allotted various duties by rotation. A particular household is assigned to keep the shroud which is used to cover the corpse during the funeral procession. The same household informs others association members whenever one of them dies. Some members are responsible for preparing the bier and carrying it to the cremation ground. Members are responsible in buying items required for the cremation. Every household is represented by at least one member in the funeral procession and at the cremation ground. In fact a roll call is taken after the cremation, and those who absent themselves frequently without valid reasons are expelled from the association. Rajendra PD. Pradhan, "Domestic and Cosmic Rituals among the Hindu Newars of Kathmandu, Nepal", p. 41.

31 In the early period there was a separate group of people known as *gons* within the *Jyapoo* caste that took the task of cremation. Nowadays, the cremation by *gons*is almost defunct and it is the *guthiyars* (*guthi* members) themselves that have taken the task of *gons*. Ajaya Kranti Shakya, op. cit., pp. 157-158.

32 Joyce Wolf Shephard, "Symbolic Space in Newar Culture" (Ph. D. dissertation, The University of Michigan, 1985), p. 182.

33 Dor Bahadur Bista, op. cit., p. 32.

Entertainment oriented *guthis*[34] are responsible in bringing *newar* communities together to organize and perform religious *Jatra*.[35] On moral level, it focuses on social harmony, brotherhood and periodic traditional community feasts; regardless of the social status or caste of the participating individual. Maintaining equality of the *newars* and fostering the feeling of togetherness is projected in this unbroken chain of *guthi* performances.[36] By keeping the traditional music and dance alive they come together and disrupt the caste hierarchy. Their participation in the *guthis* silently but truly opposes boundaries set in *newar* society. Membership to this type of *guthi* is absolutely voluntary and optional and never on caste lines. Most importantly, this type of *guthi* has no territorial boundaries.[37]

Public service *guthi* comes in the form of *toleguthi* which is established for various public services and religious purposes, such as organizing the cremation of the dead, conducting funerals, maintaining temples, rest houses, bridges, roads, public tapes and to perform *pujas* at the temples on special days or to celebrate

---

34 It promotes *Newari* culture, traditional dance and dances of gods and goddesses, cultural dresses and the traditional customs in general. In this *guthi* entertainment and religious categories are practiced by the *newars* by promoting of traditional music, musical instruments, traditional and religious dance, and cultural dressings.

35 *Nasa Guthi* and *Lasata Guthi* fall under this category. In *Nasa Guthi, Nasa Dyah*, who is regarded as a *newar* God of dance and music, is worshipped and people are trained for the religious dances and the traditional music. Deo or *Dyah Pyakha Guthi* (secret dance societies) is the only exception, which is strictly inherited and limited to certain families, and the worshipping rituals are kept secret in this *guthi*. The members have to perform the dances of various Gods and Goddesses and membership is usually passed on from father to son. Gerard Toffin, *Newar Society: City, Village and Periphery,* op.cit., p. 292.

36 Niraj Dangol, "Sana Guthi and the Newars: Impacts of Modernization on Traditional Social Organizations" (M. A. thesis, University of Tromsø, 2010), p. 25.

37 P. R. Bajracharya, *Newa: Bouddha Sanskriti Guthi* (Kathmandu: Lotus Research Center, 2008), pp. 6-10.

festivals.[38] The membership for this *guthi* is drawn from several extended family units that may include members of several caste levels and different groups.[39] Many of these *guthis* were founded by kings, their wives and rich *newars* to gain religious merit for themselves and their nominees.[40]

It is true that the *newars* have strong double-headed caste hierarchy but there are possibilities of Newar "Koinonia" and this concept of community is conveyed through *guthi* institutions. Messages of Newar "Koinonia" are evident in the practice of; (i) Common Utterances (ii) Alternative Institutions (iii) Moral Dependency (iv) Agreed Participation and, (v) Shared Role.

In 'Common Utterances' the stress is laid on the social discourses of the *newars* in *guthi* gatherings, *mandap*, *sattal* or *pati*, where they oppose inequality of religion, caste, status and de-sacralization of human dignity. In the larger domain of nepali society, hierarchy stands unopposed but this structure is challenged by the common utterances of the public. A challenge to hierarchy is to disrupt the traditional *newar* society. In common utterances, we can find the challenge of hierarchy by subordinates or common people in the streets of Kathmandu city. These common utterances are assertions for alteration and restoration of human dignity which is manipulated by a handful of upper castes *newars*. Sometimes, the common utterances are hilarious and sometimes demeaning which target the dominant group in order to abolishinhuman practices in this established structure. These utterances are contagious and that it redirects to common people for the assertion of humanity dignity. This challenge of the hierarchy is again exhibited in the playful tease as they cross each other's paths. By making hilarious utterances at the higher caste *newars*, disturbance and disorder are created in the minds of the dominant. This is considered to be a courageous act on the part of the common people for it may result in humiliation. This

---

38 David N. Gellner, *Monk, Householder, and Tantric Priest: Newar Buddhism and its Hierarchy of Ritual,* op. cit., p. 236.

39 Dor Bahadur Bista, op. cit., p. 32.

40 Rajendra PD. Pradhan, op. cit., p. 41.

informal or casual public rebellion against order and hierarchy can be a powerful source of renewal in relationships, respect and recognition. These utterances project the basic problem of inequality that is destroying the nepali society in Kathmandu valley.

In "Alternative Institutions," *guthi* institutions stand as established institutions that negate religious and caste hierarchy. These institutions bring the *newars* to a shared platform and relate in the level of religion, caste, patrilineal grouping, territory, social and public service.[41] *Newars* are expected to be members of at least two *guthis* or more in order to be members of *sana guthi* or *si guthi* and *digudya guthi. Sana guthi* serves as a platform for buddhists and hindus to come together and mutually participate in their designated roles. There are other optional *guthis* where members of various castes come together for a common religious purpose.[42] There are also *guthis* which have inter-religious, inter-caste, inter-denominational membership for the celebration of *Kumari Jatra*[43] that opposes discrimination on religious and caste lines that negate distinction between buddhist and hindu or male and female.[44] In spite of the caste, religious, social and political differences, the king, government officials, and the common people public coordinate and cooperate to undertake special roles

41 Gopal Singh Nepali, "The Newars" in *An Analysis of Nepali Culture and Society,* edited by Bishnu Prasad Dahal (Lalitpur: Adhikari Books and Stationary, 2004), p. 24.

42 David N. Gellner, *Monk, Householder, and Tantric Priest: Newar Buddhism and its Hierarchy of Ritual*, op. cit., p. 92.

43 *Kumari Jatra* is an annual festival celebrated in the Himalayan Kingdom. During this festival Goddess *Kumari* is worshipped by the nation, including the head of Nepal. *Kumari* is chosen from among the Buddhist *newar* community and installed officially. Michael Allen, *The Cult of Kumari: Virgin Worship in Nepal* (Kathmandu: Mandala Book Point, 1996); John Mellowship, *The Enchanted World of Kumari* (Varanasi: Pilgrims Publishing, 2007); Siddhi B. Ranjitkar, *Kumari: The Virgin Goddess* (Delhi: Book Faith India, 1999); Jagadish C. Regmi, *The Kumari of Kathmandu* (Kathmandu: Heritage Research, 1991).

44 David N. Gellner, *Monk, Householder, and Tantric Priest: Newar Buddhism and its Hierarchy of Ritual*, op. cit., p. 92.

in the *guthi* celebrations. From the high caste to the lowest caste, all play vital roles in *guthi* sponsored celebrations. The *Acajus* and *Karmacaryas* priests, the *Jyapoo* farmers, the *Nay* butchers, the *Jugi* tailor-musicians, the *Pode* fishermen-sweepers all involve in the *guthi* rituals.[45] It is vital to have co-ordination, participation of people from various status, religions, *phuki*, clan to ensure prosperity and harmony.[46] Participation in *guthi* celebration strengthens the inter-caste and heterogeneous structure of the *newars* and the inter-religious relations in Kathmandu valley.[47]

In 'Moral Dependency' one has to fulfill personal, societal, religious and cultural requirements demanded by *newars* ethos that display intricate connectedness in their moral domain. Their moral standards are displayed in a wide range of themes; traditional to religious and political to social. And these moral standards are intrinsically rooted in various *guthi* institutions. To a great extent, the worldview of the *newars* revolves around the moral dependency for which the impetus is derived from the *guthi* affiliations. This relationship is significant for the vibrant growth, and sustenance of the community as they continue to practice and derive meaning through various *guthi* institutions in Kathmandu valley. Perhaps, peaceful coexistence of the larger nepali society may be attributed to moral dependency asserted by the inhabitants of Kathmandu valley. Thus, majority of *newar* festivals are celebrated by hindus, buddhists, high castes, low castes, *newars* and *parbatiyas* in one accord.[48] *Guthi* institutions, which form an integral part of *newar* culture, bring the entire network of social relations and keep themselves morally dependent under this strong tradition. These closely knitted territorial units of *newar* society, small kinship units, its urban caste system and its prominent *guthi* associations are typical when compared to other groups in Nepal.

---

45 Interview with Pradip Man Shrestha, Editor, Desaymaru Jhya, 10, Maru Londegal, 25.08.10.

46 Gerard Toffin, *Newar Society: City, Village and Periphery,* op. cit., p. 333.

47 Narayan Man Shrestha, op. cit., p. 86.

48 Cf. Mary M. Anderson, op. cit.

In 'Agreed Participation' one is expected to perform cultural and religious roles. The caste system in *newar* society is a complex phenomenon where buddhists and the hindus are bound by the hierarchical order. However, the co-operation of various castes and religious groups is important for the continuation of cultural tradition that is regulated by moral order through agreed participation.[49] Here, the phrase "hamimilerajhulerabasincha" underlines the conscious choice to perform prescribed roles and sustain status quo in *newar* society. Agreed participation in *guthi* institutions is passed on from one generation to the other and thereby, establish solidarity in the society.[50] In *siguthi* members come from various *phukis* and communities. *Si guthi* pervades *phuki* (lineage), *tole* and caste divisions to perform agreed participation. Moreover, sanctity of space is important for the *newars* because this space is governed by the divine. Violation of moral order brings chaos to the ritualistic and political space which is carved out as *mandala*.[51]And the *newars* are inseparably related to each other in the cosmic order which is made possible by creating it as *mandala*.[52] For the *newars*, agreed participation in this sacred and moral space is of prime importance since it would result in earthly as well as spiritual blessings.

In 'Shared Role' the *newars* perform well coordinated roles irrespective of castes, class or religious differences which sustain the existing moral gamut of their society. All the *newars* affiliate to one or the other *digudya guthi,* where *phuki* members worship their common clan deity. Loyalty and equality of the *newars* is evident in the cultural and religious interactions each individual

---

49 Bal Gopal Shrestha, "The Newars: The Indigenous Population of the Kathmandu Valley in the Modern State of Nepal," *Contributions to Nepalese Studies*, Vol. 26, No.1 (January 1999), p. 103.

50 Niraj Dangol, "Sana Guthi and the Newars: Impacts of Modernization on Traditional Social Organizations" (M. A. Thesis, University of Tromsø, 2010), p. 25.

51 Joyce Wolf Shephard, "Symbolic Space in Newar Culture." (Ph. D. dissertation, The University of Michigan, 1985), p. 83.

52 Durga Sakya, *Hamro Sankriti Devi Tulajara Kumariko Sthan* (Kathmandu: Indrani Offset Press, 2010), pp. 87-162.

performs to establish sacred and ritualistic order. The feast organized by *Kumari guthi* is significant for group relationship, sharing and group solidarity. *Newars* affiliate to various inter-caste and inter-denominational *guthis* to share definitive roles in the celebration of national and religious festivals. In the words of Gerard Toffin, "the joint preparation and consumption of meals preceded by an act of worship is one of the principal means of enforcing the solidarity of a social group among the Newar."[53] Sharing of roles by various castes is important in this multi-caste composition. It depicts the traditional social order of Kathmandu valley without minimizing the moral ethos of *newar* society.

Conclusion

In the context of interfaith intolerance and caste hierarchy, can the *newar* community find meaning in *guthi* institutions? To a great extent, their cultural institutions promote valuable ideologies and practices that are in line with the Christian thought which present vibrant but uneasy balance. *Guthis* provide excellent platform to regulate religious and moral order in public as well as spiritual realm. *Guthis* have been instrumental in removing religious and social divide and rather, promote social solidarity. The main outcome of the shared rites is the maintenance of solidarity among the heterogeneous clan/caste structure and religious divide.[54] Thus, coming together of various *phukis*, castes, *toles*, *guthis* and religious groups is vital for the maintenance of religious and moral order. Sociologically, *guthis* provide an opportunity for the inhabitants of Kathmandu valley to pervade their marked boundaries. This phenomenon has the ability break down *phuki*, clan, caste and religious divide.[55]

---

53 Gerard Toffin, *Newar Society: City, Village and Periphery*, op. cit., pp. 301-302.

54 Narayan Man Shrestha, "Anthropological Study of Indra Jatra and Related Festivals" (M.A. Thesis, Patan Multiple Campus, Tribhuvan University, 2005), p. 88.

55 Gopal Singh Nepali, *The Newars: An Ethno-Sociological Study of a Himalayan Community*, op. cit., pp. 363-364.

Can there be resistance against the *newar* caste hierarchy that discriminates the weak, women and the powerless? I believe there can be peaceful disruptions from the informal utterances of the public in *guthi* gatherings. Further, this act of rebellion is displayed in their daily encounters between the high and the low or the pure and the impure castes. These utterances pervade religious and caste hierarchy in the social and *guthi* gatherings. 12 different *newar* castes, for instance *maharjan, khadgi, karmacarya, rajopadhyaya*, and some *parbatiyas* pervades their own boundaries during the enactment of their responsibilities in multi-caste *guthis*. These crucial interactions provide opportunities to express thoughts that builds healthy moral environment. In other words, *guthis* can be helpful models to challenge religious and caste hierarchy and related evils by exploring deep into their social and cultural institutions and ethos. It is of much significance when various class, castes and religious groups come together for diverse social and religious celebrations as it promotes mutual participations. Socially, this joint participation is important because they look after the upkeep of public water facilities, shelter houses and welfare of the common people. Religiously, they participate in sponsoring and carrying out religious *pujas* at various temples. The participation of various *guthi* members ensures the success of festivals and the fruition of public services in Kathmandu valley. In political realm, majority of the *newar* nationalist organisations are making positive effort by accommodating members of all castes in their organisations.[56] While political parties may have their own agenda in making the membership open to all castes and yet, it does not underestimate the importance of bringing people together to equal pedestal. Peaceful religious co-existence, prosperity, respect, dignity, loyalty among the *newars* can be established when the principles of *guthis* are practiced in the right moral spirit.

---

56 Bal Gopal Shrestha, "The Newars: The Indigenous Population of the Kathmandu Valley in the Modern State of Nepal," …p. 103.

9

A Better Way Forward for Peacemaking and Prevailing in the Multi-Religious Context of India
A Missiological Perspective

Jayakumar Ramachandran[1]

Introduction

Almost all countries in the world have a religiously pluralistic populace; some countries are constitutionally secular whereas 'others' are not. 'Others' are constitutionally inclined to either 'religious'[2] or 'non-religious'[3] phenomena. In all countries, tolerance toward other religious worldviews is decreasing. This results in intolerance toward others' religious beliefs and faiths. Episodes of religious conflicts between the Dalai Lama and the Republic of China, Shia and Sunni Muslims, *Bodu-Bala-Sena* and Muslims in Myanmar and Sri Lanka, Muslim Fulani Herdsmen and across sub-Saharan Africa, Fanatic Hindus and Muslims, and conversions and reconversions in India are unending.

---

1 Rev. Dr. Jayakumar Ramachandran is the Founder of Academy for Church Planting and Leadership and the General Secretary and Director of Indian Institute of Inter Cultural Society; he is also a member of Evangelical Theological Society and Evangelical Missiological Society.

2 Islamic (ex: Saudi Arabia), Jewish (ex: Israel), Christian (ex: Brazil), Hindu (ex: earlier Nepal), and Buddhist (ex: Sri Lanka) nations.

3 China and North Korea.

Religious intolerance issignificantly increasing in contemporary India as it never has before, despite this Land having given birth to four religions and enshrined both secularism and freedom of speech in its constitution. Harmony in the country is devastated by various issues and significantly by 'conflicts between religions'. Making peace prevail amongst people of religious diversity is the challenge of the hour. Appreciable efforts to organize interfaith dialogue have been made by numerous national and international agencies in past history. Did these efforts build harmony among multi-religious Indians and make peace prevail? How can harmony be built in order to let peace prevail among people of diverse schools of belief and faith in this multi-religious Land? Coward's assessment is noteworthy;

> Hindu-Christian dialogue has had a long and checkered history. Up until the beginning of this century most Hindu-Christian interaction took place in India. The first half of this century saw the expansion of Hindu-Christian discussion to Europe and North America. Worldwide pluralism in the decades since the fifties has resulted in a gradual intensification of this interaction at both the lay and scholarly levels. But there has been no broad and sustained Hindu-Christian dialogue. (*Coward 1993, 1*).

This paper focuses primarily on finding solutions for two primary unknowns: (1) What kind of efforts would result in a constructive peacemaking and peace-prevailing atmosphere in the multi-faith context in India? (2) How do Christians who are called to be the salt of the earth and light of the world and commissioned to 'make disciples of all nations' respond to the challenge of plurality of religion in India? To make my insights perceivable, the following observations and suggestions are presented.

Presuppositions

The following presuppositions are the foundation for the development of my thoughts in this paper:

(1) Presently, in post-modern and multi-religious India, most people believe that no single religion, belief system

or theology has any impeccable claim to be exclusive. Pluralism is gaining rapid prominence.

(2) India is a democratic nation. Every individual has the right to believe, promote and defend their religious beliefs, values, and practices. The spirit of freedom of religion is to protect every religion by providing freedom to every religion.

(3) Religion has a key role in the power play of Indian politics. Religious beliefs and political power are being intentionally interwoven by fanatic communities. Religions are used for enhancing voter turnout by exploiting religious sentiments for political gains.

(4) Constitutional provision of secularism and religious freedom are loosely worded and so legislation and judiciary play key roles in interpreting them.

(5) The Christian Church is called to be wise, pure and sacrificial as it fulfills God's Mission (Matt. 10:16, "Behold, I am sending you out as sheep in the midst of wolves, so be wise as serpents and innocent as doves.").

(6) There is one Truth and many lies. Lies are the outcome of futility and blindness of people's minds (Rom. 1:18-23). The pre-requisite for inducting the Truth is a peaceful relationship with those who have not recognized it.

(7) The Mission of God provides opportunities for every person on earth to receive eternal and earthly blessings. God used even unbelieving people for accomplishing His Mission in the biblical historical narratives.

(8) Dialogue should not be limited to 'table discussions'.

(9) Dialogue does not necessarily lead to dilution of faiths, values and practices of any religion.

I believe that interfaith dialogue can build effective bridges of cooperation between religious and philosophical traditions. However, would that make people of diverse religions live peacefully in harmony, giventheir distinct faiths, values, and practices? And in particular Christians, who are 'called' to be the salt and light of the world and mandated to 'make disciples of all nations' and in need of bridging congruent connections with people of other faiths.

Core Purpose of the Mission of God

What is the Mission of God and why is it so? A description has not been precisely published. Since it is God's mission, originating in God's mind, human perception still lags in understanding this fully. The Mission of God is a 'comprehensive solution' for all the problems of mankind for all time. It is God's solution for remaking all 'good' what He created for everyone's good; a solution to straighten up the fallen world. It was an apt solution for the first man in his situation and indeed as well as for the readers of this day.

A simple exegesis on certain passages in the scriptures becomes essential to perceive the vital purpose of God's solution – His Mission. Paul writes in 2 Corinthians 5:18-19, "Now all these things are from God, who reconciled us to Himself through Christ and gave us the ministry of reconciliation, namely, that God was in Christ reconciling the world to Himself, not counting their trespasses against them, and He has committed to us the word of reconciliation". Setting aside all hotly debated issues related to second Corinthians, I would encourage the readers to consider Paul's plain communication in this section. The Reconciled are made to be the reconcilers and to reconcile others with God and one another. Paul's exhortation reminds the Corinthians about the unique reconciliation made, by which; (1) an eternal relationship is established between the ungodly community, who exercised their belief in His death on the cross for salvation, and God, and (2) entrusted the same ministry of reconciliation to the saved community to enhance the 'reconciled community' in the world. The entrusted ministry of reconciliation to Christians has both vertical and horizontal dimensions. Paul elaborates, "For he himself is our peace, who has made us both one and has broken down in his flesh the dividing wall of hostility by abolishing the law of commandments expressed in ordinances, that he might create in himself one new man in place of the two, so making peace, and might reconcile us both to God in one body through the cross, thereby killing the hostility" (Eph. 2:14-16).

God's mission activity always brings 'peace' between God and fallen humanity and thus makes a harmonious community of the people of God. The purpose if His mission is to make sure that peace prevails between God and man and among all men. The angel prophetically heralded, "Glory to God in the highest heaven, and on earth peace to those on whom his favor rests" (Luke 2:14). Isaiah prophesied, "But he was pierced for our transgressions, he was crushed for our iniquities; the punishment that brought us peace was on him, and by his wounds we are healed" (53: 5). Healed here is restoration. These prophecies, though they have immediate relevance to the people of Israel, also have implications for all mankind, and this cannot be denied.

Jesus said as He was sending His disciples, "As the Father has sent me, even so I am sending you" (John 20:21), where the mission of the disciples is modeled on the mission of the Son. The Mission of Jesus involves both proclamation and service, individual and communal renewal, justification and justice and peace with God and peace on earth. Failing to come fully to terms with this comprehensive nature of mission is a failure in mission itself.

He was sent for reconciling man with God and man with man. Disciples are 'sent as' Jesus was sent. In the phrase *kathos,* the adverb not only qualifies the verb *apestelken* but also derives significance from it; *apo* + *stello* means "sent on a defined mission by a superior". From Paul's understanding, the mission was 'to promote peace provided in Jesus' for the world. Peace talked about in the New Testament is crucial to understanding Jesus, salvation, the mission of the church and eschatology. (Swartley 2006, xi). Since the cross of Jesus, the centrality of *Missio Dei,* was to accomplish 'Peace', therefore the Christian community – the Church- should commit to "Peace" promotion. The vital purpose of *Missio Dei* is to promote and establish 'Peace' as provided in Jesus. The Triune God, 'the God of peace' (Romans 15:33), sent His son to die on the cross to make peace prevail between God and man and among the people of this earth. The gospel therefore is 'the gospel of peace', (Eph. 6:15) which is the message to be proclaimed the centrality of the Mission of God.

For Luther, mission is always pre-eminently the work of the triune God, and its goal and outcome is the coming of the Kingdom of God (Scherer 1987, 55). The Kingdom is the sphere of life where God's Spirit is in control; where justice, peace and joy are experienced completely and permanently as found in Rom. 14:17 (Kirk, 1999, 29).

Origin and Appraisal of Interfaith Dialogue for Peacemaking and Peace Prevalence

Akbar the Great made efforts to promote tolerance in the 16th century among the people of various faith backgrounds in ancient India. In the early 20th century interfaith dialogue started to take place between Christianity, Judaism, Islam and *Bahai.*[4] The first interfaith dialogue was initiated by Jules Monchanin (1895-1957) and then by Dom Henri Le Saux known by his monastic name Swami Abhishiktananda (1910-1973) of Tiruchirappalli. They initiated intense dialogue with Hindus. Their work in dialogue, which began with great courage but in isolation within the Church, has paved the way for the work of dialogue in India today. Further, P.D. Devanandan (1901-1962) who was the cofounder and the first director of the Christian Institute for the Study of Religion and Society had provoked rich and original thinking in the field of dialogue. Subsequently, Vatican Council II for the first time valued non-Christian religions and has led the Church's position regarding non-Christian religions. On Pentecost Sunday, 1964, Pope Paul VI instituted a special department of the Roman Curia for relations with the people of other religions. Know at first as the Secretariat for non-Christians, in 1988 it was renamed the Pontifical Council for Interreligious Dialogue (PCID) (Pontifical Council for Interreligious Dialogue). In 1969, an All India Seminar

4 The Bahai is a monotheistic religion, founded by Bahaullah in 19th-century Persia, which believes in unity of all humanity and religions, practices, prayer, reflection and serving the community.

on the 'Church in India Today' was held at Bangalore which set encouraging guidelines for the pursuit of dialogue with Hinduism and other non-Christian religions.

The Roman Catholic Church issued the Vatican II document *Nostra Aetate* in 1965, instituting major changes in the Catholic Church's policy towards non-Christian religions. In 1978, the Interfaith Conference of Metropolitan Washington was created to bring together eleven historic faith communities to promote dialogue, understanding and a sense of 'community' among persons of diverse faiths. The Interfaith Youth Core is the most recent group formed by Eboo Patel, an American Muslim by religion, for building relationships, mutual respect and recognizing religious pluralism. Efforts in the past made by some Christian theologians, such as Bede Griffiths, known as Dayananda, Raimundo Panikkar, M. M. Thomas, Pierre Fallon, Samuel Ryan, Sebastian Kappen, D.S. Amalorpavadass, George Soares Prabhu, Francis D'Sa and Hindu theologians Swami Chidananda of Sivananda Ashram, Swami Bhajanananda of Ramakrishna Mission and Swami Veerendra Heggade, the head of the Dharmasthala Math in South India are noteworthy. Present efforts being made by the Jesuit's Snehasadan, Poona (Pune), Universal Peace Federation, New Delhi, The Student Christian Movement of India, Inter Church Service Association, YMCA India, Ramakrishna Mission, Islamic Fiqh Academy, India, Henry Martin Institute and many others deserve appreciation.

Whenever religious conflicts arise, proposals for dialogue increase. Interfaith dialogue and peacemaking efforts in a multi-religious context are very sensitive in nature. However, societal living and integration among people is indispensable. On the other hand people-uniqueness cannot be dismissed. Integrated disintegration, or unity in diversity, or unity with no uniformity – would this be possible? Every religion makes claims for its uniqueness and exclusiveness. A clear sense of the uniqueness of a religion combined with a willingness to explore and visit other world faiths without destroying them, are central ingredients in religiosity that is oriented to peacemaking.

Interfaith dialogue that is aimed at recanting or bracketing the claims of religious uniqueness of any religion will not achieve its purpose of peacemaking. It should have a single agenda, which is peacemaking that leads to establishing reconciliation and respect between bodies based on human rights, societal ethics, and wider justice. Thus, I define peacemaking as an action to identify and support structures which will tend to strengthen and solidify peace to avoid relapsing conflicts. Hence, interfaith dialogue should be defined within this purpose of peacemaking. By doing so, it would lead to a positive and cooperative interaction between people of different religions, faiths or spiritual beliefs, with the aim of promoting understanding between different religions thereby increasing acceptance and tolerance. Constructing dialogue between followers of different religions means understanding the different religious principles and teachings that would benefit all of humanity through the promotion of mutual respect and tolerance. This does not mean that uniqueness of their respective religious faiths and beliefs should be shuffled to make a new syncretistic school of faith; nor to renounce their mission, which is part of their faith. Distinct faiths and practices do not breed conflict; rather it is the result of the mode by which religious people do it. The mission of a faith is not the conflict point, it is the way in which mission is executed that generates skirmishes.

Interfaith dialogue should not intend to take away or brush aside respective and distinct faiths and practices of other religions nor should it aim at coming to a common and syncretized belief. It rather should seek to accomplish a mutual recognition and understanding of 'other' faiths and beliefs to build good relationships between religious schools, as people are expected to live in harmony in any given community of a region."Interreligious dialogue is sustained conversation between parties who are not saying the same thing and who recognize and respect contradictions and mutual exclusions between their various ways of thinking" (Taylor 2007, 102).

A mature lecture from Dr. Uma Mysorekar, a practicing gynecologist and a key leader of the Hindu Temple Society of North

America, at the UN Special Event on *World Interfaith Harmony: Multi-religious Partnership for Sustainable Development* is noteworthy for Christians to understand the vitality of interfaith dialogue.

> The term interfaith dialogue refers to the positive and cooperative interaction between people of different religious faiths and spiritual beliefs, with the aim of promoting understanding between different religions to increase acceptance and tolerance. The power of religion can be used as a major force of unification among divergent factions and hence it can play a key role in the promotion of global peace and reconciliation by bringing various groups together. (2015)

Interfaith dialogue indeed breaks down the barriers and stigmas which lead to distrust, suspicion and bigotry.

Role of the Church in Building Harmony and Peacemaking in India

Many Christians consider interfaith dialogue as an offensive act against their Christian faith, mostly due to those who, in their desire to create harmony among various religions, are found compromised with the essentials of their own faith. Until the recent past, not many Christian churches and organizations extended their interest toward interfaith interactions. Without diluting the vitality and uniqueness of Christian faith and calling, they can still seek ways in which interfaith interactions for peacemaking and peace-prevalence could be achieved.

The UN General Assembly is comprised of 193 member states of distinct political policies, religious adherences, economic and developmental status, and other legacies. This unique forum is meant for multilateral discussion of international issues, in particular, peace and security. Eachcountry's distinctions remain untouched. They have unity without uniformity and unity in diversity. Christians who disagree with interfaith dialogues should look at the functional reality of the General Assembly of the UN.

Since the Church is an agent of God to minister to the people at large in the context of a pluralistic society, Christians are called to incarnate the Truth by means of togetherness, sympathy, solidarity and cooperation toward their neighbors. Their presence in living together with other people of faith for fellowshipping, serving, and sharing of the good news of Jesus cannot be accomplished unless a strong relational bridge is built through dialogue.

The spiritually profound Hebrew word shalom, 'peace', which is God's peace, not only speaks about the 'harmony with God', but also that access to the 'good life', a life in which God's good intentions for humanity are being realized. Shalom denotes the absence of conflict or war which is a necessary condition for human embellishment. The Greek usage of the word 'eirene' speaks of 'a state of national tranquility' or 'exemption from the rage and havoc of war' apart from the peace that would come through the Messiah. Radical missiologist Hoekendijk who defined evangelism contrary to the term that is historically used, sees firstly Messiah – Christ himself - as the subject of evangelism, and, therefore, secondly, the aim of evangelism is nothing less than what Israel expected the Messiah to do, i.e., establish shalom (1967, 19-20).

The Church is called to peacemaking as her non-debatable mandate, and has to promote the 'Peace' that comes through the Messiah. Impeccable and perfect peace indeed would come and prevail through the Messiah in eternity. However, a mandate should not be limited to preaching on the 'Peace that would come eschatologically'. The Church needs to initiate establishing peace on earth by eradicating rage, enmity, animosity, and disharmony. The Eternal God came in flesh to demonstrate God to mankind. Eternal peace needs to resemble and then be promoted on earth among the human society of His followers.

Jesus, who had come to renew the Jewish Law, despite being considered as an enemy of the Law by his contemporaries, remained available for dialoguing with them. Jesus was found doing the same with Nicodemus in a friendly manner on religious matters in spite of his identity as a Pharisee. Despite the hostility between Samaritans and Jews dating from Israel's split, the existence of sharp religious schisms among them, and arguably each condemning the other as heretics, Jesus made a friendly connection with the Samaritan woman. Heaven portrayed the Samaritan in the parable as 'good' in Luke 10:25-37. Peacemaking is found in the Sermon on the Mount, "Blessed are the peacemakers, for they will be called the sons of God" (Matt. 5:9). Jesus does not talk about peaceful, peace-keepers, or peace-loving people, instead he talks about people who defuse hostility and build bridges, resolve conflict and seek concord, combatants for peace who pull down walls of hostility. Jesus' use of the terms in the consequent passages in Matthew is noteworthy; opponent (5:42), gentiles (5:47; 6:7; 6:42), enemies (5:43 – 44), unrighteous (5:45) and persecutors (5:10 – 12 and 44). These clearly indicate that peacemaking is not restricted to the sphere of believers alone rather it extends to the entire unbelieving world which is beyond the boundaries of the Church.

Paul exhorts the believers in Rome to remain at peace with their fellow citizens (Rom. 12:18). The author of the book of Hebrews insists that Jewish people living in Rome need to take every effort to remain at peace with their fellow citizens of other religions and beliefs (Heb. 12:14).

Need for Broad and Sustainable Peacemaking and Peace-prevailing Efforts

In general, interfaith dialogue is intended to bridge the gap between people-divides and to form societal coalitions in order to challenge the bloodshed, fear, turmoil, and injustice generated by the dynamics of religious fanaticism. It should be a means to prevent conflict between communities and thereby decrease the potential for people-divides. Numerous dialogues have taken place in history as this paper has mentioned in the introductory section. What did they accomplish? In July 2008, Saudi King Abdullah, while opening an Interfaith Conference in Madrid, said, "Most of the dialogue between religions has ended in failure". What has interfaith dialogue accomplished in India?

In spite of various efforts made by different agencies, including the Church at large in India, peace is not prevailing among the religious communities. The key findings of the 2016 report by the United States Commission on International Religious Freedom, place the strongest emphasis on deteriorating religious tolerance and increasing violence in India, according to the Indian Express dated 3 May 2016 (which was then denied by the Government of India). Ram Navami violence in Hazaribagh, Jharkhand, (reported 18 April 2016, in the Indian Express) is another illustration in the history of religious intolerance in the country. Arundhati Roy's returning of her National Award, (reported 5 Nov 2015 in the Indian Express) and Nayantara Sahgal's returning of her Sahitya Akademi award (reported on 22 Jan 2016 in the same daily) are other illustrations of the reality of increasing intolerance in the country.

When religion is fueling communal violence and a repulsive atmosphere, a need for a strategically designed approach to peacemaking and its careful implementation are inevitable. Such broad efforts will certainly be a sustainable solution. In the light of the status of religious tolerance it becomes inevitable to evaluate the ongoing phenomena and proceedings of interfaith dialogue in the country. Evaluation requires gauging the phenomena, motives, goals, operational methods, and the overall outcomes.

Setbacks in Dialogue Strategy

What are the causes for the failure of the present dialogue methods in achieving religious harmony in India? Efforts in dialogue that have taken place thus far truly deserve appreciation. It is an undeniable fact that unrest prevails in general between religious segments in the country. The following four setbacks are some of the key possible reasons for the partial ineffectiveness of dialogue in the past.

Setback of Limitations in Dialogue: Dialogue means a meeting point between the logos. Etymologically, dialogue denotes conversation between two or more individuals or groups. Epistemologically, dialogue connotes a common point where all faiths can meet, and therefore, interreligious or interfaith dialogue means conversation between people of different faiths or religions. In such interactions, the motives of dialogue vary from event to event, such as solving polemical issues, mutual knowledge, reconciliation and many others.

Setback of Questionability in Reaching a Friction-free Meeting Point: In my opinion I do not think that at any time in the past or even in the future, religious faiths can meet at one friction-free point. There are many doctrinal similarities and dissimilarities among religions. Yet absolute similarities are seldom found. The monotheistic religions - Judaism, Christianity and Islam - agree that there is a sole God, but their understanding of the 'nature of God' and the 'nature of Jesus' is dissimilar. Although, some varieties of Hinduism count many deities as aspects of a single God other strands of Hinduism are henotheistic, worshiping one deity but recognizing many others. A meeting point is likely possible only when absolute similarities are found in doctrines of various religious schools. Hypothetically, even if absolute similarities are found in certain doctrinal beliefs, would this be concluded as a constructive meeting point for 'peacemaking' among multi-faiths? Unless dissimilarities are made peacefully agreeable by the adherents, peacemaking and peace-prevalence cannot be accomplished.

Setback of Diversity of Beliefs and Values: Religious pluralism is a reality that is part of the human society in countries like India where religious freedom is constitutionally granted for every individual. One group of people or an individual's most fundamental and cherished assumptions about the best way to live may differ radically from the values held by another group or individual (Pearce 1997, 49). It is a phenomenon in which epistemology and anthropology are found combined. Even if hypothetically the world had happened to have a single religion, plurality of thoughts among that single religious people would be inevitable and would keep generating divides among mankind.

Setback of Down-Flow: Religious conflicts are primarily not from religions. Most of the conflicts are from the societal factors such as diversity of castes, economic status of people, cultural values, political leanings, and various other upheavals related to the real-life context of the people. The conclusions that are reached in dialogue are normally limited to the drafting of declarations. How strongly do they down-flow to the lower tiers of people groups? Conflicts are not found basically among the elites who sit around the dialogue tables. In reality, most of the religious dialogues are being carried out by the elite representatives of society. I was invited to a dialogue in Chennai where 15 other iconic leaders of other faiths also took part. After various issues regarding religious violence had been discussed, representatives expressed their desire to work toward amicable relationships between religions. The key observation was that the representatives that took part in this dialogue were mature leaders of their respective schools of faith; they had no conflict issues amongst themselves. People in grassroots groups, who are two or three tiers below the elites, are the ones who have been the subjects of conflicts. Since the efficacy of our dialogue did not trickle down to the lower tiers of community, the impact of the dialogues was limited.

Setback of other Hidden Sources Unhandled: There are considerable evidences for the outbreak of civil conflicts apart from religious fanaticism such as poverty, social divisions, political grievances (Blattman 2010, 45), and cultural autonomy (Gautam, 1994). Other blind spot is politicized motives of politicians who bait 'favors' to certain religious people with anticipation of a positive reciprocation eventually ends up with communal clashes. Conflicts based on these hidden causes often colored as religious conflicts. In the light of the prevailing religious hostility and intolerance in India, I am confused about the efficacy of interfaith dialogue as a solution. So, what should be the way forward?

Way Forward

Our dialogues are far away from real peacemaking. Peace among a few dialoguing people in limited phases is not real peacemaking. Peacemaking is about building peaceful, stable communities and societies (Schreiter 2002, 4). Its aim is to prevent violence and destructive conflict, heal individuals and societies from the effects of hurts and reconcile individuals and communities in order to live harmoniously in the future in multi-religious India. Peacemaking demands conflict resolution, promoting nonviolent-activism, balancing human rights, rectifying constitutional ambiguities and societal development. In order to find a way forward for harmony and peace among multi-religious people, I would first of all outline some of the undergirding issues, which need to be addressed.

Work on Erasing Misconceptions about Other Religions: A considerable number of Hindus believe that the Christian faith is from the West; invariably they connect the Christian faith with *Dalits* as they responded positively to the mission efforts of the missionaries in the past; thus faith in Jesus Christ is stigmatized with 'foreign' and 'untouchable' adjectives. Since Hinduism is polytheistic in its nature, there are many Hindus that consider Jesus as one of their gods, yet find it unacceptable when Jesus comes as part of the Christian-religion package. This is a misconception. On the other side, there are many Christian teachers, preachers and leaders who present the Hindu religion as 'Demonic'. This misconception eventually led them to incorporate many strained, hostile and offensive words and phrases toward Hindus and the Hindu religion. Emerging Islamic fanaticism is leading many non-Islamic religious people to stigmatize Islam as a brutal religion. Many Christian teachers and preachers present Islam as a counterfeit religion to Christianity. Since many Hindus connect Islam with beef-eating, they consider Islamic people as their enemies. When the five pillars of Islam were governing their basic beliefs (*Shahadah*, *Salat*, *Sawm*, *Zakat*, *Hajj),* in the late 20th and early 21st centuries, extremists began declaring the concept of *jihad* as the sixth pillar to rationalize and legitimize terrorism, under the banner of 'protecting' Islam from all other ungodly forces against Allah. These misconceptions are not obvious among elites. But the truth of the matter is that these misconceptions are still hibernating in many elites, even among those who participate in interfaith dialogue. Fanatics of all religious schools pour fuel on these conceptions for their own ends. This truth is also reflected in the Constitution of the United Nations Educational, Scientific and

Cultural Organization (UNESCO), in the statement, 'ignorance of each other's ways and lives has been a common cause, throughout the history of mankind' for suspicion and mistrust through which their differences have 'all too often broken into war'.

Establish Mutual Trust: Various hidden realities produce fertile mutual trust between the religious adherents. Conversion episodes tagged with the conversion agenda of Christian mission agencies and churches remain a threat to non-Christian religions. More than conversion, the consequences of conversion, which include alienation from cultures, families, and identities, are the threats. Conversion also threatens the Hindu religious people as it makes Christians and Muslims move higher in the population scale. The retaliating counter-action of reconversion episodes initiated by fanatic Hindu segments and being supported by many Hindus is considered as a threat by the Christian community at large. This threat is increasingly intensified by the activities of the present ruling party at the Center, which is obviously pro-Hinduistic. Speeches delivered by key proponents and their intimate acquaintance with the Hindu sadhus and gurus intensify the threats among the non-Hindu adherents. Inhuman terroristic attacks executed by Islamic fanatic groups also generate threats among non-Islamic religions.

Make Efforts to set Right Ambiguities in Constitutional Provisions: Freedom of religion makes Christians work aggressively for conversion of people to the Christian faith; pro-Hindu political agencies, as a counter-action to the conversion agenda of Christians, have been reconverting Christians to the Hindu faith. Conversion agenda and reconversion episodes generate unrest among Christian and Hindu religious segments at large. One of the causes of the prevailing ambiguity among Christians and Hindus in relation to 'religious freedom' is the imprecisely defined words and phrases in certain articles of the Indian constitution.

Incompletely defined words and phrases in the Indian constitution, such as Article 25, have been paving the way for executing anti-conversion law in many states.

Make Efforts to Remove the Hidden Detriments in Constitutional Provisions: Provision of special clauses for 'minorities', which is under scrutiny by the pro-Hindu ruling party, is interpreted as an anti-minority act by the minorities. The battle between 'sharia' and religious freedom is as yet unsettled; the denial of the scheduled caste benefits for converted Christians from other faiths is unsolved. These setbacks in interpreting constitutional provisions remain as obstacles to peacemaking and retaining peace among the various religions adherents. A need for amicable settlements in precisely defining constitutional provisions of minorities is the undeniable solution.

Discourage 'religious extremism': Indeed, some of the religious extremists in association with political power promote intolerance and discrimination. Religious extremism will make any country susceptible to being a latent source of conflict; association of political power will cause eventual conflict escalation. As long as people entertain 'religious extremism', efforts toward 'peacemaking' will achieve only a futile end. It is high time for all the religions in India to discourage any form of 'religious extremism' in their respective regions.

Promote "Brotherhood" Innovatively: Presently-growing international interactions, global access and travel possibilities, the mixture of peoples and ethnic and religious groups in various societal sectors, and modern and advanced technical means of communication, have collectively caused religions to interact with each other at large. It is apparent and obvious to on lookers that religions and the societal components will not go together in complete harmony. In order to build harmony and peace I would challenge the religious leaders to consider promoting 'brotherhood' vigorously among their respective populace. The Brotherhood I advocate is not a resulting consequence of an amalgamation of religions of distinct people but rather a state of 'a feeling of shared interests and support among all humans' (Cambridge Dictionary) which would pave a way for people to recognize their fellow citizens with dignity and respect, irrespective of their creeds and cultures. Brotherhood efforts that were made in the past by different religious schools and organizations at different times of history did not achieve much. The Preamble to the constitution of India declares that the constitution would promote fraternity. *Frater* the root Latin word for fraternity means 'brotherhood'. Sixty-five years away from the adoption of the Constitution of India, Indians cannot claim any credit for having promoted the mission of fraternity in their country (Varghese 2015, 51).

Response to the Issues

Responses are suggested here under two subtitles. The first subtitle "The General Response", makes suggestions to all the religions in general; the second subtitle "A Christian's Response", contains suggestions exclusively for Christians.

Do more than Dialogue: India needs a broader and a far more mature interfaith interaction, which I would name as "Peace Makers Meet", and by doing this we make our focus to be solely set on peace making. This identity will make all people-tiers of various religious communities understand the core objective.

Apart from dialoguing, innovative measures are to be invented to build harmony among the religious communities. It was found in a study on 'the ethnic conflict among Hindus and Muslims in India', that in Indian cities where Muslims and Hindus have opportunities to engage regularly with one another there is less likelihood of inter-communal violence breaking out in the face of political, economic or social disruptions.

Towns where Hindus and Muslims continue to be integrated – in businesses, political parties, unions, professional associations of lawyers, teachers, doctors and students, and clubs – are also towns where riots are either absent or rare. An integrated organizational and civic life makes the state behave much better than intellectual and political exhortations that it does (Varshney 2002, xi).

Setting sports events in every region wherein the teams comprise members from different religious beliefs is an ideal strategy to promote harmony. Ideal illustrations are Indian cricket, hockey, football and kabadi teams which consist of players from different religions, but play the sport in unity. Religious factions are not highlighted as they play for the Nation; inter-religious spectators admire the inter-religious players.

When Chennai was flooded a couple of years ago religion was forgotten by people at large. Muslims were helped with passion by Hindus; Christian churches extended help to non-Christians. It was an ideal display of religious harmony in an adverse, calamitous situation. Common philanthropic human issues cause a community to set aside their religious differences. Therefore, common human problems and issues allow a multi-religious community to set aside religious identities. There are many housing societies in Gujarat where Hindus and Muslims work together for common good.

Enhance Participant Representations beyond the Religious Leaders: Since religious disharmony is also based on various hibernating non-religious issues and challenges, peacemaking and peace prevalence should include politicians, legislators, and even fanatical leaders as the issues are discussed. There are incidents designated as a 'religious conflict' which, however, have a non-religious cause. For example, Mitra and Ray (2010, 720) show that differential economic growth between Hindus and Muslims can generate conflict, due to resentment over relative economic well-being.

Seek for Representations from all Tiers in the Society: Up to this point dialogue is prevalent among elite icons. This needs to be extended to all levels of communities in India.

Chapters for 'peace making and peace prevailing' should be made to actively function in every sub-urban, village, and tribal region.

Educate to Respect People of Other Faiths: Religious institutions in every region should come forward to educate their students about other religions. Hindu institutions should take the initiative to educate their adherents to treat adherents of the Christian faith with appropriate respect and recognition. They should educate their adherents not to treat Christianity and Islam as foreign, unpatriotic or as a religion of the Dalits.

Hostility toward 'other faiths' is the outlook for some Christians. One of the key reasons for their resentment is their "mission motive and method". 'Other faiths' are unfortunately pictured before Christians as the enemy's scheme against the Church. Thus, mission motive for some was made to be an act of extracting people from 'other faiths' through their so-called evangelistic battles; they describe other faiths as a demonized phenomenon, deserving militant action by the Church. The Bible does not say other faiths are demonic. Churches must educate Christians not to be disrespectful and offensive toward other faiths.

The peacemaking need in society infers an existence of conflicts or enmity between two communities. Though not all Hindus and Christians have unsettled conflicts, yet conflicts between them are undeniable. Investigation of who is the cause for the existing conflict will mar the peacemaking efforts. The reason for it being unsettled would be a good investigation. It is unsettled as many Christians are yet vigorously fanning the flame of animosity instead of making efforts to achieve the core purpose of the mission of God, which is peacemaking. Peacemaking efforts will pave a constructive way for a relationship, which ultimately will turn to be a gateway for fulfilling the mandate of 'making disciples of all nations'. Reconciling their mandate of 'making disciples of all nations' and the multi-religious reality in India are two extremes which have to be reconciled. How should Christians respond to this challenge?

Repentance will Initiate Peacemaking: Churches, agencies and individuals should come forward to repent of their abusive and hurtful words and deeds toward Hindus and their worldviews imbedded in their religion. They should be mindful of the 'honor and shame' context. Christians may interpret their actions as positive, yet they might inadvertently shame people. Logical actions from one frame of reference can create barriers to relationships when interpreted from a different frame of reference. For example, extraction of a new believer from cultural and religious contexts generates pride to the Christian missional community and shame to the respective family members of other faith. Bridges with the community cannot be restored unless the Christians recognize the honor/shame context where they are called to "make disciples".

Efforts to make the Church Distributed into Society will pavea Way for Constructive Peacemaking: The World is frantically looking for charismatic saviors with purity, love, passion, idealism, comfort, care, forbearance, patience and morale. Christians should recognize that they are called to be the salt and light of the world. There are many avenues of need in society where the Church can offer tremendous service to the non-Christians of India. Hunter writes:

> In the present model of the church, the local church tends to be isolated and preoccupied with its own world. It appears to be, and often is self-centered. God in Christ came out of His self-sufficiency to identify with those radically different from Himself, and His church is called to be like Him. The church that is distributed values ministry beyond its walls more than ministry inside them because it focuses on those not yet included. It reaches through relationships it has within its congregation to identify with others. Intentional distribution of the church with a goal of ultimate connection through relationship reflects God's image (2007, 13).

The Church is being considered by the non-Christian communities as a religious cage trap. I do agree that there is some truth in this debatable outlook. The Christian mission is not only to show what they have in the churches or where we will spend eternity; it is also to demonstrate before society what Christians can do for humanity in an unselfish manner. This would lead to interfaith relational bonds at the grassroots which interfaith dialogues do not always do as they often fail to 'down-flow' to the lower tiers of people. Make every effort to present churches as 'centers for comfort and counsel' for the neighborhood instead of appearing before them as cage-trap devices. The Church must be considered as a community of unselfish benefactors committed to the holistic wellbeing of the community.

Practicing the Christian Faith and Mission Cautiously will sustain Peace Inter-religiously: Most Christians interpret Article 25 of the Indian constitution as an unconditional provision for freedom to worship, propagate and profess their faith. They have to remember this freedom is for every religious community in India. Total freedom for multiple communities will lead to conflicts. There is a need for a legitimate mechanism aimed at neutrality. Article 25 is of this sort. It does not give total and absolute freedom to any religion. Freedom is subject to order and morals. Having this attitude not only will protect Christians by legal clauses but also would sustain peace with fellow religious communities. In 1 Corinthians 9:19-20 Paul says, "For though I am free from all men, I have made myself a servant to all, that I might win the more; and to the Jews I became as a Jew, that I might win Jews". His testimony is to tell us how cautious he was as he served among 'others'. His testimony, as well implies two advantages of being 'cautious'– (1) he was able to protect himself from the religious and political hierarchies and (2) he could communicate the Truth to his hearers.

Conclusion

This paper cannot claim to be an absolute solution for the disenchanting religious-relational context prevailing in India. My thoughts are intended to communicate to the readers that peace making and peace-prevailing are quite possible in India among multi-religious people without hindering their respective epistemological uniqueness. This paper appreciates the interfaith dialogues that have taken place in the past but meanwhile comments that peacemaking and peace-prevailing cannot be achieved by mere dialogue. Since my suggestions toward the problem presented still need further thought, I challenge emerging theologians and missiologists to explore more on the subject in order to find better means and ways for peacemaking and peace-prevailing in our great country of India.

10

Truth and Reconciliation Commission, South Africa A Model for Peace and Reconciliation in Kaduna State, Nigeria

Yakubu Tanko Jakada[1]

Introduction

The Truth and Reconciliation Commission, in South Africa was a laudable project praised internationally for bringing healing and reconciliation to those oppressed under the regime of apartheid in South Africa from 1948 to 1994. Many South Africans like the people of Kaduna State in Nigeria were wounded, heart broken and tortured. The once peaceful state with its symbolic peaceful river has been plagued by violence which has forced the emergence of settlements along religious division which is an unfortunate situation.

That the bitterness, distrust, tension and anger can literally be smelled in the air underscores the need for peace and reconciliation. It is hoped that the lessons learnt from the Truth

1 Yakubu Tanko Jakada is a faculty of the Baptist Seminary Kaduna Nigeria, he attended the International Peacemakers Program of Hartford Seminary, Hartford, Connecticut USA, and currently doing his PhD work in Intercultural Studies at Asbury Theological Seminary Wilmore, Kentucky in the United States.

and Reconciliation Commission in South Africa will go a long way in helping to achieve lasting peace in Kaduna State.

Apartheid in South Africa

Before the arrival of the whites in the seventeenth century, the Khoikhoi or Hottentots were in South Africa. The Portuguese sailors in 1554 reported seeing the people of the land, 'very black in color with wooly hair.'[2] The painting on caves in the Cape area is an added testimony to prove that the whites are not the original inhabitants of South Africa.[3]

The word 'apartheid' is an Afrikaans word meaning, 'the state of being apart.'[4] The word is used for every kind of segregation against the civil rights of citizens due to ethnic prejudices by a state or country.[5] Apartheid was established and nourished on a faulty theology of superiority in human creation and false "philosophy of 'scientific racism' that it was impossible, impracticable and ungodly for different races and cultures to live as one."[6]

The ascendance of power of the Afrikaans whose ancestors were Dutch colonists in 1948, made the blacks and people of color experience different kinds of segregation and oppression. Daniel Malan was the first apartheid Prime Minister. Oliver F. Williams outlined some of the oppressive sanctions against the blacks from 1948-1960. Below is an excerpt from Williams;

Legal Sanctions

From 1948 until 1960s, the legislature of South Africa passed major laws that formed what became apartheid.

---

2 Oliver F. Williams, *The Apartheid Crisis* (San Francisco: Harper and Row Publishers, 1986), p. 24.

3 *Ibid.*

4 David M. Smith, *Update: Apartheid in South Africa* (Cambridge: Cambridge University Press, 1987), 10.

5 *Ibid.*

6 Eugene P. Dvorin, *Racial Separation in South Africa* (Chicago: Chicago University Press, 1952), 41.

1949: Prohibition of mixed Marriages Act: This law forbids intermarriages. In 1950, it included sexual acts between whites and blacks. It was repelled in 1985.

1950: Population Registration Act: All South Africans are to be classified according to racial categories.

1950: Group Areas Act (amended 1966): The key stone of separate development; this divided zone land by race. The black Land act of 1913, the Development Trust and the Land Act of 1936, provided some 14% of the land to the ten 'homelands' for Africans.

1952: Abolition of Passes and Coordination of Document Act: The 1952 Law coordinated existing pass laws and required that all Africans age 16 years or over must carry a reference (pass) book at all times. The pass book indicates whether the holder has permission to be in a white designated area.

1953: Bantu Education Act: The Act was intended to ensure that the educational system reflect the government policy of separate development.

1953: Reservation of Separate Amenities Act: This law- along with a number of others- provides for wide range social segregation- cinemas, buses, trains, taxis, libraries, schools, beaches, resorts are segregated.

1956: Labor Relations Act: This Law reaffirmed the principle that certain skilled jobs would be reserved for the whites.

1959: Extension of University Act: The Act forbade a white University to admit black students unless the course of study sought by the student was not available at a black University.

1959: Promotion of Bantu Self-Government Act: The bill provided that the small part of the country that has been set aside as native areas or Bantu home lands be divided into eight (now ten) 'self governing' national units of Bantustans. All blacks, on the basis of tribal heritage, would be assigned to one of these homelands, and voting rights would be exercised there rather than in the national parliament.[7]

---

7 Williams, *The Apartheid in Crisis,* pp, 35-39.

Painful and Traumatic Experiences of Apartheid in South Africa

South Africans went through painful experiences in their land. According to the limit of this paper, a few of the experiences shall be highlighted.

The Pass Laws were humiliating experiences to black South Africans who were expected to carry a Pass Book while moving in their land as if they were slaves. The Dutch colonial Governing Authority passed this law in 1797 extending the law beyond slaves to include the Khoikhoi (Hottentots) when moving about the country for any purpose.[8] This was to check the movement of the black majority who had been allocated only 14% of the total land area. In the words of Desmond Tutu, the Pass Laws, "more than anything else in South Africa demonstrated that the black person is a second class citizen in the land of his birth."[9] It was painful.

There were indiscriminate arrests of people said to have violated the Pass Laws. Students going to school and men coming back from work were arrested. The police were given power in 1967 to detain opponents of apartheid indefinitely without access of family, solicitors or courts.[10] Allen A. Boesak gave an account of the painful arrests thus, after four years of state of emergency, after the violence that caused the repression. You remember that within the first eighteen months of the state of emergency, more than 50,000 people were put in prison-without charges, without trial 40% of them were children under 18 years old. During that state of emergency we saw an eight-year-old, a 10-year-old and a 12-year-old children being detained. Mothers taken away from their children and kept in jail and others gave birth in jail-without ever being charged.[11]

---

8 Smith, *Update: Apartheid in South Africa*, 15.

9 Desmond Tutu, *Crying in the Wilderness* (Grand Rapids, Michigan: William B. Eerdmans Publishing Company, 1984), pp. 72-73.

10 Ibid., 69.

11 Allen A. Boesak, "South Africa Yesterday, Today and Tomorrow." *Vital Speeches of the Day*. Vol. 56, Issue 15 (Presented, 05/15/96), p. 464.

The arrest of Nelson Mandela with other African National Congress leaders sentenced to life imprisonment in 1964 was painful to the blacks of South Africa.[12] The killing in 1960 of 69 people by police in Sharpeville,[13] the brutal killing of Steve Biko, the leader of the Black Consciousness in 1977,[14] the protest of the Youth of Soweto against being taught in medium of Afrikaans of which the police opened fire and killed some of them.[15]

The forced eviction and resettlement of blacks under the homeland system where they will no longer be citizens of South Africa, but foreign migrant laborers on temporary permit is part of the painful experience.[16] Ten homelands were allocated to different black ethnic groups; Labowa (North Sotho), Qwaqwa (South Sotho), Boputhatswana (Tswana), Kwazulu (Zulu), KaNgwane (Swazi), Trasnkei and Ciskei (Xhosa), Gazankulu (Tsonga), Venda (Venda), and KwaNdebele (Ndebele).[17] As a result of the resettlement, husbands had to leave their wives and children to go in search for work as migrant workers in white man's town, living an unnatural life in a single-sex hostel, prey to prostitution, homosexuality and drunkenness.[18] This was a deliberate attempt by the whites to break up families of the blacks.

With the separation of settlements, came separate developments, separate education and separate amenities such as buses, trains, parks, libraries, etc. The standard of the whites is

---

12 http://www.southafrica.info/about/history/history.htm#.UOofl1vdu18 (accessed 04/13/14).

13 Njongonkulu Ndungane, *A World with a Human Face* (Geneva: WCC Publications, 2003), p. 1.

14 http://www.southafrica.info/about/history/history.htm#.UOofl1vdu18 (accessed 04/13/14), ii.

15 Ibid.

16 Smith, 52.

17 Ibid, 36-37.

18 Desmond Tutu, "After Word: A Christian Vision of the Future of South Africa." Christianity Amidst Apartheid. Martin Prozesky ed. (New York: St. Martin's Press, 1990), p. 233.

often higher than that of the blacks.[19] There were certain skilled jobs and businesses that were reserved for the whites.

Whatever goes up must come down. On 2 February 1990, F. W. de Klerk lifted restrictions on 33 opposition groups including ANC, the PAC and the Communist Party. On February 11, Mandela was released after 27 years in prison.[20] There was a democratic election won by the ANC and Nelson Mandela was sworn in as President on May 10, 1994. This ushered in a new South Africa.

The Truth and Reconciliation Commission South Africa

The Truth and Reconciliation Commission was established to deal with the legacy of the apartheid period. It was a court like body established in 1995 by the South African Government to help in healing the country and bring about reconciliation and uncovering the truth about human rights violations of apartheid period.[21] The emphasis was not to prosecute individuals but to gather information and evidence from victims and perpetrators. That is what made it different from Numberg trials that prosecuted Nazis after World War II.[22]

Geiko Muller-Fahrenholz outlined the objectives of the TRC as;

(1) Establishing as complete a picture of the causes, nature and extent of the gross violations of human rights which were committed during the period from March 1, 1960, to cut-off date, including the antecedents, circumstances factors and contexts of such violations, as well as the perspectives of victims and the motives and the perspectives of the persons responsible for

19 Smith, 15-16.

20 http://www.southafrica.info/about/history/history.htm#.UOofl1vdu18 (accessed 04/13/14).

21 Desmond Tutu, Truth and Reconciliation Commission South Africa. Available at http://www.britannica.com/EBchecked/topic/607421/Truth-and-Reconciliation-Commission-South -Africa-TRC (accessed April 10, 2014).

22 Ibid.

the commission of the violations by conducting investigations and holding hearings.

(2) Facilitating the granting of amnesty to persons who may make the full disclosure of all the relevant facts relating to acts associated with political objectives and comply with the requirements of this Act.

(3) Establishing and making known the fate of the whereabouts of victims and restoring the human and civil dignity of such victims by granting them an opportunity to relate their own accounts of violations of which they are the victims, and by recommending reparation measures in respect of them.

(4) Compiling a report providing as comprehensive an account as possible of the activities and findings of the commission which contains recommendations of measures to prevent the future violations of human rights.[23]

The TRC's important feature was its openness and transparency. It assured that in the public hearing, South Africans became aware of the atrocities that had been committed during the apartheid years.[24] The commission released the first five volumes of its final report on October 29, 1998, and the remaining two volumes of the report on March 21, 2003.

Challenges and Limitations of the Truth and Reconciliation Commission

Excerpts from Desmond Tutu's article in Encyclopedia Britannica on the TRC reveal the following challenges;

- Not all parties to the conflict accepted the TRC.

---

23 Geiko Muller Fahrenholz, The Art of Forgiveness (Geneva: WCC Publications, 1997), pp, 85-86.

24 Desmond Tutu, Truth and Reconciliation Commission South Africa. Available at http://www.britannica.com/EBchecked/topic/607421/Truth-and-Reconciliation-Commission-South -Africa-TRC (accessed April 10, 2014).

- Top military officers did not cooperate with the commission.
- Senior politicians in the apartheid government did not apply for amnesty.
- It was difficult to get the liberation movements to participate in the amnesty process on the ground that they conducted a 'just war' as such they do not need to apply for amnesty.
- The amnesty to be given to be granted the perpetrators of evil during the apartheid regime was seriously challenged. Desmond Tutu defended it as being part of the package of initiatives contained in the interim constitution that set the country on the road to becoming a democratic, constitutional state as such, South Africans have to learn to live with the compromise.[25]

Assessment of the Truth and Reconciliation Commission

Desmond Tutu in his article made the following assessment of the TRC.

- The TRC is internationally regarded as successful.
- The first commission to hold public hearing in which both victims and perpetrators were heard.
- It laid foundation for building reconciliation among all South Africans.
- The South African TRC has provided the world with another tool in the struggle against impunity and search for justice.

Ethno-Religious Violence in Kaduna State, Nigeria

Kaduna State is one of the 36 states of the Federal Republic of Nigeria located in the North-West Geopolitical zone. Kaduna State experienced bloody inter-communal clashes and massacres. The most deadly riots took place in 2000 and 2002 which left many thousands dead. Below are the notable ethno-religious conflicts in the state.

---

25 Ibid.

(1) Kafanchan Religious Violence- 1987: Violence erupted in Kafanchan in March 1987 at the College of Education over an interpretation of a Qur'anic verse by a Christian preacher invited to preach in the annual mission conference organized by the Fellowship of Christian Students. The violence spread to Kaduna city and the northern parts of the state. At least 19 people died, 152 Churches and 5 Mosques were destroyed. A special tribunal was set up by Kaduna State Government, 75 persons were convicted, but before the trial was completed, the tribunal was asked to stop.[26]

(2) Zangon Kataf Violence-1992: In February and May 1992, violence exploded between Atyab (Kataf) predominantly Christian people group and Hausa-Fulani Muslims in Zangon Kataf town, Southern Kaduna state.[27] News of the massacre in Zango sparked reprisal killings in Kaduna city and northern parts of the state. Of the 1,833 that died in this violence, 1,528 died in Zango alone. The town was reduced to rubble. Some arrests were made and about 21 persons were convicted and sentenced to death. The death sentence was later reverted to five year imprisonment.[28]

(3) Shari'a Riots- 2000: On February 21, 2000, the Christian Association of Nigeria Kaduna branch organized a protest march against the introduction of Shari'a (Islamic Law) in Kaduna State. A reaction from Muslim youth resulted in violent clashes in February and May, it was reported that about 2,000 people were killed.[29] There was wide spread destruction that left the city in rubbles. Dead bodies of the victims were taken to eastern Nigeria; the Igbos took revenge on the Hausa-

---

26 Ibid.

27 http://www.hrw.org/node/121279/section/9 (accessed April 15, 2014).

28 Books.openedition.org/ifra/761 (accessed April 15, 2014).

29 Obed Minehakpu "Chronic Violence Claims 2,000 Lives" Christianity Today. Vol.46 No. 1 (Jul. 2002), p. 23.

Fulani and massacred several hundreds of them. In the two cases, about 500 were arrested and charged to court.[30]

(4) Miss World Riots- 2002: In the year 2002, when Nigeria was to host the World Beauty Contest, an article was published, in a Lagos based Newspaper, 'This Day' about the pageant which was provocative to Muslims, a protest by Muslim youths turned violent, some Christians were, killed, with their homes, business premises and Churches burnt. The Christians retaliated and also killed Muslims, burnt their homes, business premises and Mosques. Some 250 people were killed in Kaduna alone. Apart from some possible summary convictions, leading mostly to fines, no one was convicted for crimes committed during either the 2000 or 2002 riots.[31]

(5) Post Election Violence: Northern Nigeria and Kaduna State in particular in the after mirth of the April 2011 peacefully conducted elections which is judged to be the most free, fair and credible election in Nigeria both by local and international observers was visited by bloody violence. Hundreds of people died and properties worth millions of Naira destroyed.[32] The violence erupted following the declaration of the Presidential election. A presidential committee on 2011 Election Violence and Civil Disturbance was set up and headed by Sheikh Ahmed Lemu. The committee submitted her report on 20th May 2011.[33]

---

30 http://www.hrw.org/node/121279/section/9 (accessed April 15, 2014).

31 Ibid.

32 Nigeriavillagesquare.com/forum/main-square/63390-assessment-post-election-violence-swept-kaduna-some-northern-states-nigeria (accessed April 16, 2014).

33 http://www.academia.edu/4653367/PRESIDENTIAL-ELECTION-RESULT-AND-POLITICAL-VIOLENCE-IN-KADUNA-NIGERIA (accessed April16, 2014).

Pains, Trauma and Need for Healing

The experiences of religious and ethnic violence in Kaduna State over the years have caused deep seated hurt, pain, anger, bitterness, animosity, etc. Friends and relatives have been killed leaving many women widowed and children orphaned. Properties worth millions of Naira was destroyed, some sections of cities and towns reduced to rubbles.[34] Places of worship burnt, destroyed and or desecrated. Many families who were well to do were reduced to penury. Many had to put up with the pains of becoming refugees in their own country that is not at war, others were compelled to leave the towns or villages where they were born in to settle in other places and start life afresh.[35]

Many people in Kaduna State are living in fear and tension, distrust and suspicion. People move to areas they feel secure, towns and cities are getting more divided along religious lines.[36] Hearts are wounded! Hearts are hurting- There is need for healing, hence the study on the miracle of healing and reconciliation in South Africa with the hope that the lessons learnt from the TRC of South Africa will help in securing lasting peace in Kaduna State and Nigeria and any community in any part of the world having similar experiences.

Lessons from the Truth and Reconciliation Commission South Africa

(1) The decision to establish the Truth and Reconciliation Commission was not a unilateral decision. It went through a wider consultation involving different segments of the society. Desmond Tutu wrote, "Civil society, including human rights lawyers, the religious community, and victims, formed a coalition of more than 50 organizations

34 http://www.voanews.com/content/wave-of-violence-sweeps-central-Nigeria/1844905.html (accessed April 20, 2014).

35 http://www.endtimeschristianity.com/cgi-bin/webbbs-config.pl?noframes;read=68 (accessed April 20, 2014).

36 http://www.bbc.com/news/world-africa-20141305 (accessed April 20, 2014).

that participated in a public dialogue on the merit of a truth commission. This consultative process lasted a year and culminated in legislation, the promotion of National Unity and Reconciliation Act 34 of 1995 (the Act) that established TRC."[37]

(2) This process is very good because if people participate in the formation of an initiative, they will be committed to it.

(3) Negotiation and Compromise: The African National Congress under Nelson Mandela that was engaged in arms struggle for the liberation of black South Africa had to arrive at a decision to discontinue arms struggle and engage in negotiation. In this negotiation, they had to reach a compromise and amnesty was part of the compromise. It is a known fact that arm struggle has never achieved permanent peace but negotiation had, the case of South Africa is a practical example.

(4) Victim Orientation: The TRC focused primarily on the victim. Victims were treated with respect, people stood up when they came in to testify. The victims were given opportunity to relate their painful memories in their language. There was freedom of expression, no harassment and victims were sure of their security after they testify. Material assistance was immediately given to families who were more badly affected. The TRC finally recommended reparation for victims.

(5) Investigation avoided a kind of witch-hunt: The purpose of the commission was reconciliation and national unity. The past was genuinely looked into in order to have peaceful and safer future. The investigation cut across all races and political affiliation.

(6) Amnesty: Given to South Africans both white and black who applied and are prepared to give detailed account of their activities and prove beyond doubt that their acts were

---

37 Desmond Tutu, Truth and Reconciliation Commission South Africa. Available at http://www.britannica.com/EBchecked/topic/607421/Truth-and-Reconciliation-Commission-South -Africa-TRC (accessed April 10, 2014).

politically motivated. Those who qualified were given amnesty.

Conclusion

This paper wishes to draw the following conclusions:

(i) The TRC succeeded because it had the input of different stake holders in the society. It was not just the wish of one person or a few leaders, but the decision of the community. When government decides what the community's need is and hand pick the members of the committee that will handle the peace process, manipulation is inevitable as can be seen in the case of the 1987 Kafanchan violence.

(ii) The TRC's priority on 'Victim Orientation' is praise worthy. Many Peace and Reconciliation projects are initiated in some contexts in order to placate some individuals or groups and some times used as tools for personal vendetta. Those types of peace initiatives end up with reports and recommendations that do not have any positive impact on the victim.

(iii) Amnesty is good but not practicable in all cases. There is need to study the problem thoroughly and decide whether amnesty is appropriate or not. In the case of South Africa, it was a compromise that the black South Africans had to accept and the TRC did well to have kept the promise to grant amnesty.

Recommendations

The writer wishes to recommend the followings to the Government of Kaduna State:

(i) Whenever there is conflict among communities in the state be it ethnic or religious, there should be a true and unbiased assessment of the remote cause of the conflict. This will help the committee to give just and fair recommendations.

(ii) Victims of the crisis should be the main priority of the peace and reconciliation process not political leaders, parties or some segment of the society.
(iii) Victims of crisis should be helped immediately. Adequate compensation should be given to victims.
(iv) The law should be given primacy in the state. There should be no sacred cows who should be perpetrating evil with impunity. Those who perpetrate evil and their sponsors should be punished.
(v) Corruption that has caused abject poverty among the masses has been one of the major causes of violence in Nigeria. The wealth of the nation should be evenly distributed in the provision of infrastructures, social amenities and jobs for young people. (vi) The Government should be proactive against future occurrence of ethno-religious crisis by engaging in public awareness campaigns, seminars, constant meetings with religious and ethnic leaders to promote peace in the state.
(vii) The Government should endeavor to look into the needs of the minorities whether religious or ethnic who feel marginalized or oppressed.
(viii) The Government should not be afraid to go into negotiation and if possible compromise if doing so will bring about peaceful co-existence.

11

Some Basics Features of Interfaith Dialogue

Toshi Aier[1]

In a world that is increasingly becoming religiously intolerant, interfaith dialogue has become essential in order to help people discover, celebrate and promote the reality of pluralism. It is important that people respect and have appreciation for other's faith traditions. In dialogue we hope to build relationships, identify commonly-held beliefs and enhance the participants' own faith experience. Simply stated, interfaith dialogue involves meeting people themselves and getting to know their faith traditions. The most common form of interfaith discussion is when two individuals, be they friends, neighbours, or acquaintances, discuss their religious beliefs in a casual setting. Calvin Shenk calls this 'living dialogue.'[2] These discussions can be very valuable in promoting better understanding of the different religions that make up our pluralistic society. While valuable, however, such discussions do not constitute formal interfaith dialogue.

More formally, it consists of "discussions for mutual understanding held among differing religious bodies."[3] Paul F.

---

1 Mr. Toshi Aier teaches History of Christianity at Clark Theological College, Aolijen, Mokokchung.

2 Calvin E. Schenk, *Who Do You Say That I am?* (Scottdale: Herald, 1997), 210.

3 Donald K. Mckim, *Westminster Dictionary of Theological Terms* (Louisville: WJP, 1996), 147.

Knitter describes interfaith dialogue as "the interaction of mutual presence, speaking and listening, witnessing the commitments, the values, and the rituals of others."[4] Perhaps, the best definition of interfaith dialogue comes from John Taylor who states that, "Interreligious dialogue is a sustained conversation between parties who are not saying the same thing and who recognize and /respect contradictions and mutual exclusions between their various ways of thinking."[5] Similarly, what Lochhead says is very apt in regards to the function of dialogue- "Rather than defining dialogue as a search for *agreement*, it would be more helpful to define dialogue as a search for *understanding*. To understand another tradition, I do not have to agree with its precepts. I do not have to create 'common ground' in order to proceed."[6] The primary function of interfaith dialogue should be to promote greater understanding between people of different religions.

"The experience of people who have come into deep dialogue with those of other faiths is that it more deeply enriches one's sense of oneself."-Diana Eck

"My fundamental belief is that all religious traditions have the same potential to make better human beings, good human beings, sensible human beings, compassionate human beings." -Dalai Lama

Modes of Dialogue[7]

While the nature of dialogue may differ from place to place depending on the time and situation, most organized efforts adhere to a particular type of dialogue. Several distinctive, yet interrelated modes have emerged over the years. Let us briefly look at some of them.

---

4 Paul F. Knitter, *Jesus and the Other Names* (Maryknoll: Orbis, 1996), 14

5 John Taylor, "The Theological Basis for Interfaith Dialogue" in *Faith Meets Faith*, ed. Gerald Anderson and Thomas Stransky (Grand Rapids: Eerdmans, 1981), 94.

6 Lochhead, *The Dialogical Imperative* (Maryknoll: Orbis, 1998), 60.

7 This section is borrowed from Laji Chacko, *Christian Response to Multi-Faith Issues* (Kolkata: Scepter, 2016), 172-73.

'Parliamentary dialogue' is carried on by large assemblies convened for interfaith discussions, the earliest example of which was the 1893 World's Parliament of religions in Chicago. Such gatherings became more frequent in the late twentieth and early twenty first centuries under the auspices of multi-faith organizations such as the World Conference on Religion and peace and the World congress of Faiths. These sessions tend to focus on better co-operation among religions and the challenges to peace to all.

'Institutional dialogue' is the organized effort to initiate and facilitate various kinds of dialogue meetings. In addition to the immediate focus, this approach also seeks to establish and nurture communication between institutional representatives of religious organizations. Institutional dialogue encompasses much of the work carried out through the Vatican and the WCC, with numerous variations at the local level.

'Theological dialogue' includes structured meetings in which theological and philosophical issues are the primary focus. It also refers to discussions on the meaning of one's religious tradition in the context of religious pluralism.

'Dialogue in community' and 'the dialogue of life' are inclusive categories concentrating on the practical. Issues of common concern such as peace and harmony, development, relation with the state, education, rights of minorities, etc., are central. This type of dialogue is often designed to encourage common action. Another important function of this dialogue is to generate intentional and informal daily interactions among the adherents of different religions.

'Spiritual dialogue' is concerned with developing, nourishing, and deepening spiritual life through interfaith encounter. Considerable space for spiritual exploration is possible here-from observing the worship to sharing in the festivals and celebrations of each other, to a bolder initiative such as joint worship experience.

It is important not to assume that one particular mode of dialogue is the only legitimate one. The context must govern what kind of dialogue is most appropriate within a particular local sense. We may need many different strategies for developing dialogue amongst and between communities.

Nature of Dialogue

There are many things to discuss on the nature of dialogue but let us limit to only a few as we prepare to enter into dialogue. *Firstly*, dialogue has to be truly two dimensional or else it is not true dialogue. It will be monologue. Dialogue is also not debate. We do not enter into dialogue to argue our position. *Secondly*, we must understand that dialogue is a process, not a product. It requires the building up of trusting relationships. It may begin in any situation but gradually allow natural human relationship to flourish. *Thirdly*, in dialogue there is going to be discomfort and tension. Courage is needed to work at the edges of our discomfort. *Fourthly*, Humility is a key ingredient in dialogue. One cannot enter into dialogue with a preset notion of superiority and right. *Fifthly*, communication is not just the matter of using words. It is also about presence and example. Sometimes shared silence, exploring one another's character in the silence and being prepared to listen before we speak to one another are part of the real two way dialogue. *Sixthly*, in all types of dialogue encounters there will be differences in terms of thinking, feeling, and action. We need to develop enough capacity to hold those differences so that we can dialogue on them in an effective, creative and a productive way.[8]

Levels of Interfaith Dialogue

1. The dialogue of life, where people strive to live in an open and neighborly spirit, sharing their joy and sorrows, their human problems and preoccupations.
2. The dialogue of action, in which persons of all religions collaborate for the integral development and liberation of people.

8 Ibid., 173-4.

3. The dialogue of theological exchange, where specialists seek to deepen their understanding of their respective religious heritages, and to appreciate each other's spiritual values.
4. The dialogue of religious experience, where persons, rooted in their own religious traditions, share their spiritual riches, for instance with regard to prayer and contemplation, faith and ways of searching for God or the Absolute.

Almost similar to the above, but with slight variation, we can also understand the levels in this way;

1. Informational: Acquiring of knowledge of the faith partner's religious history, founding, basic beliefs, scriptures, etc.
2. Confessional: Allowing the interfaith partners to speak for and define themselves in terms of what it means to live as an adherent.
3. Experiential: Dialogue with interfaith partners from within the partner's tradition, worship and ritual – entering into the feelings of one's partner and permitting that person's symbols and stories to guide.
4. Relational: Develop friendships with individual persons beyond the business of dialogue. Practical: Collaborate to promote peace and justice.

Concerns in Dialogue

The first concern is a lack of focus. For any interfaith dialogue to succeed, all parties must be clear on the conversation's goals. This can help people decide which conversations they should join. For example, if the goal is to discuss complex theological issues, it is necessary to include scripture experts, historians, linguists, and other academics. Normally, lay people may not feel comfortable in these discussions. On the other hand, conversations focused around personal values and experiences would be more appealing to them or to people who are less interested in theology. Academics who want to debate religious minutiae would probably shy away from these discussions. Thus, it is necessary to hold multiple different types of conversations, each geared to a different audience.

The second concern is when people feel that they need to 'water down' or compromise their religious identity in order to fit in. This often occurs when dialogue participants come across an irresolvable difference. Ideally, interfaith dialogue is supposed to not only help each other but also help each participant better understand their own religion and discover the areas in which their religion is unique. In the situation described, both parties should agree to disagree. They should accept that differences exist and seek to understand them without compromising their own beliefs.

The third concern is proselytizing or attempting to convert others. This is also antithetical to the idea of respecting each other's differences. It is perfectly acceptable for dialogue participants to claim that they have the absolute truth. After all, many religions make similar claims that often conflict with beliefs of other religions. However, in interfaith dialogue, participants should enter the conversation in order to learn about other religions' beliefs, not to promote their own. Although, there may be a time and place for proselytizing, interfaith dialogue should not be done with conversion in mind.

Interfaith dialogue can be an excellent way to heal divisions in society. Social science research indicates that having a positive, meaningful relationship with someone of a different background and learning about their identity correlates to viewing that person's entire group more favourably. The same logic applies with interfaith conversations. If we pursue interfaith dialogue while attempting to address the challenges described above, we can break down stereotypes and find more areas of common ground.

Challenges to Interfaith Dialogue

There are different challenges of varying degrees posed to interfaith dialogue. In India today we talk of three of the greatest concerns that are posed before interfaith dialogue. They are;

Religious Fundamentalism- Religious fundamentalism poses a great threat to peace and harmony all over the world.

Today, religious fundamentalism is raising its monstrous head in varying degrees in almost all religions in all the corners of the earth. No religion is exempt. What Martin E. Marty has observed is quite true. He says, "Fundamentalism looks backwards and set out to freeze some moment, some event, some text or texts from the past as the perfect place in time or space from which to measure."[9] A close scrutiny of religious fundamentalism reveals some basic fundamental presuppositions common to all. They are-*firstly*, absolute claims. Fundamentalism is all about absolute claims-only one truth, one God, one interpretation. This brings about superiority and inferiority, right and wrong. This also gives absolute power to the person who interprets the religious text/s. *Secondly*, The superior-inferior, right-wrong dichotomy creates exclusivism and authority and whoever is not part of the authority is excluded. Those who are part of the authority try to impose their conviction upon others by all ways and means. *Thirdly*, exclusive claims lead to the negation of others. The other is devalued and dismissed and termed as rival or competing alterity, faith, ideological or otherwise.[10] *Fourthly*, once the preceding sets of factors are in operation, it is but a short step towards sanctioning imposition and legitimated extremism. Any insubordination is resulted in destruction.[11]

Politicization of Religion- As religion come to occupy more and more critical space in politics and public life, politicization of religion has become a pervasive phenomenon in many parts of the world. Religion becomes a weapon in the struggle for political power and domination. Applying the concept of religion is highly problematic in this context because is subordinated to politics. This is xenophobic construction of politicized religion. Political goals actually assume primacy over religious doctrine. In other words, political goals are formulated first and then religious ideas and symbols are mobilized to enhance achieving these goals.

9 Martin E. Martin, *Fundamentalisms Compared*, 1.

10 Douglas Pratt, "Terrorism and Religious Fundamentalism: Prospect for a Predictive Paradigm" in *Marburg Journal of Religion,* 11/1 (June, 2006), 12.

11 Ibid., 12-13.

The problem is in the assumption that political parties are only successful if they invoke religious identity during elections.[12] Religion thus becomes a dividing force in social and political arenas in a more intensive and durable form.

Religionalization of Politics- The flip side of politicization of religion is the religionization of politics, the impact of which has not been always identified.[13] The religionization of politics leads politics to pander to the interest of religious groups who would like to influence and control political power. In order to establish absolute authority of their own claims a strong grip on political power is a must therefore fundamental groups use politics for religious purposes. The strategies used by certain religious groups are to devise and carve roles for themselves in politics by way of invoking religious sentiments against other minority religious groups. At the same time, they position themselves as true champions of their religion which is 'under threat' from minority religions and their foreign affiliations.

When politicization of religion or its reverse takes place, relations between different religious communities are increasingly impacted by changes in local and national politics which have been largely reconfigured along particular religious lines. The politicization of religion and the rise of religious extremism in our country and elsewhere mutually reinforce each other. It not only poses a threat to religious freedom of the adherents of minority religions, but the survival or religious minorities is affected.[14]

Interfaith Dialogue in the World Council of Churches

It can be truly said that WCC had been responsible for the emergence of an organized dialogue movement[15] when it began, in the 1950s, to organize a number of formal meetings between Christian leaders and representatives of other religious traditions.

---

12 Laji Chacko, *Christian Response*, 151.

13 Statement on the Politicization of Religion and Rights of Religious Minorities, WCC 10th Assembly, Document No. PIC 02.1.

14 Ibid.

15 Laji Chacko, *Christian Response,* 192.

These efforts resulted in the formation of new interfaith institutions. Towards the later part of the Vatican Council II, Pope Paul VI established a Secretariat for Non-Christian religions to study religious traditions, provide resources, and promote interreligious dialogue through education and by facilitating local efforts by Catholics.

Since its inception in 1948, it has been the desire of the WCC to open dialogue with other religions which resulted in the establishment of the program *Dialogue with People of Living Faiths and Ideologies* (DFI) in 1971. This program supports inter religious multi-lateral and bilateral dialogue with partners of different faiths. It has become an important instrument in expressing that "Christians today live out their lives in actual community with people who may be committed to faiths and ideologies other than their own."[16] It also implies that dialogue "be recognized as a welcome way of obedience to the commandment of the Decalogue; `you shall not bear false witness against your neighbor', not to disfigure the image of our neighbors of different faiths."[17] WCC also recognized that those committed to other religious traditions are 'people of living faiths'. By doing so, it invites Christians to reflect afresh on what God may be doing in the lives of hundreds and millions of men and women who live and seek community together with Christians, but along different ways.[18]

The Central Committee of the WCC understood the engagement of the world Council in dialogue as a common *adventure* of the churches (Italics mine). The word adventure takes on several meanings at once. It may mean a hazardous or even questionable undertaking, but it may also signify an unusual or exciting experience. The issue of interfaith relations and dialogue in the history of the WCC resonates with both meanings of the word adventure. Interfaith dialogue has always been and

16 WCC Guidelines on Dialogue with People of Living Faiths and Ideologies, 1979.

17 Ibid.

18 Ibid.

continue to been closely scrutinized. Some Christians fear that such dialogue is equivalent to syncretism or a fusion of religions, but there have also been others for whom dialogue is a way to constructively acknowledge religious plurality and look for ways to take today's context seriously. More than ever, we sense a growing need not just for dialogue with people of other faiths but for genuine relationships with them. Increased awareness of religious plurality, the potential role of religion in conflict and the growing place of religion in public life, presents urgent challenges that require greater understanding and co-operation among people of diverse faiths.[19]

Of the numerous documents that have been formulated in relation to dialogue in the WCC over the years, let us take a cursory look at two which I think are important for us.

1. ***Guidelines on Dialogue***: Guidelines on dialogue between people of different faith commitments have come from all over the world that often reflect quite different situations. Very often they are what is called as 'bilateral' in their scope, referring to what should happen between just two partners in a conversation. Other sets of guidelines are 'multilateral' and tend to refer to the general principles involved in interfaith encounter. One such multilateral guidelines is the WCC's *Guidelines on Dialogue with People of Living faiths and Ideologies* formulated in 1971 and reworked in 2002 as *Ecumenical Considerations for Dialogue and Relations with People of Other Religions.*[20] This important statement underscores four principles of dialogue;

1. Dialogue should proceed in terms of people of other faiths, rather than of theoretical impersonal systems.
2. Dialogue can be welcomed as a way of obedience to the commandment of the Decalogue; "You shall not bear false witness against your neighbor".

19 Ecumenical Considerations for Dialogue and Relations with People of Other religions, WCC, 2002.

20 Kenneth Cracknell, *In Good and Generous Faith: Christian Responses to Religious Pluralism* (Cleveland: The Pilgrim Press, 2006), 99-102; 127.

3. Dialogue is a fundamental part of Christian service within community.
4. The relationship of dialogue gives opportunity for authentic witness.

The guidelines also affirmed that, "We feel able with integrity to commend the way of dialogue as one in which Jesus Christ can be confessed in our world today; at the same time we feel able in integrity to assure our partners in dialogue that we come not as manipulators but as genuine fellow pilgrims". The last sentence reveals the *metanoia* (repentance) and humility that are necessary ingredients of dialogue.

2. ***Christian Witness in a Multi-Religious World***:[21] This document was the outcome of the third consultation in 2011 and jointly issued by the Pontifical Council for Interreligious Dialogue (PCID), the World Council of Churches (WCC), the World Evangelical Alliance (WEA) as a set of recommendations for conduct on Christian witness around the world.

Study the issues set out in this document and where appropriate formulate guidelines for conduct regarding Christian witness applicable to their particular contexts. Where possible this should be done ecumenically, and in consultation with representatives of other religions.

Build relationship of respect and trust with people of all religions, in particular at institutional levels between churches and other religious communities, engaging in ongoing interreligious dialogue as part of their Christian commitment. In certain contexts, where years of tension and conflicts have created deep suspicions and breaches of trust between and among communities, interreligious dialogue can provide new opportunities for resolving conflicts, restoring justice, healing of memories, reconciliation and peace building.

Encourage Christians to strengthen their own religious identity and faith while deepening their knowledge and understanding of different religions, and to do so also taking

21 http://www.vatican.va/christianwitnessinmulti-religiousworld.

into account the perspectives of the adherents of those religions. Christians should avoid misrepresenting the beliefs and practices of people of different religions.

Cooperate with other religious communities engaging in interreligious advocacy towards justice and the common good and, wherever possible, standing together in solidarity with people who are in situations of conflict.

Call on their governments to ensure that freedom of religion is properly and comprehensively respected, recognizing that in many countries religious institutions and persons are inhibited from exercising their mission.

Pray for their neighbors and their well being, recognizing that prayer is integral to who we are and what we do, as well as to Christ's mission.

The above shows that interfaith dialogue is a serious issue undertaken in the WCC. How we practically apply the dialogue guidelines and recommendations to our local context depends on us.

In an increasingly pluralistic world, dialogue becomes the means of bridging people of diverse faiths together. It enhances our sensitivity regarding the faith of other communities. It allows people of different faiths to arrive at mutual understanding and respect that permit them to live and cooperate with each other in spite of differences. Let our dialogue today bring us together as members of one's humanity and let us be passages of God's Shalom to one another.

Editor & Contributors

Rev. Dr. Mar Pongener teaches History of Christianity at Clark Theological College.

S. Dhane Zhemai is Lecturer of the Department of Old Testament, Witter Theological College, Wokha.

Woba James is an Associate Professor and HoD of History of Christianity at Eastern Theological College, Jorhat, Assam.

Shanbha Hayong is an Associate Professor, Department of Theology and Ethics at John Roberts Theological Seminary, Mawklot, Shillong.

Eyingbeni Hümtsoe-Nienu teaches Christian Theology and HoD of the Department of Christian Theology, Clark Theological College, Mokokchung, Nagaland.

Rongsen Longkumer, Professor of Christian Ethics taught at Clark Theological College, Mokokchung till 2016.

Prabhakar Bhattacharyya is Associate Professor & Head Philosophy Department, Serampore College.

C. Pursenla Ozukum is a Doctoral Student in Religion under South Asia Theological Research Institute (SATHRI), Senate Serampore College.

Dhanbir Rai teaches Religion and the Dean of Post Graduate Studies at Clark Theological College, Mokokchung, Nagaland.

Jayakumar Ramachandran is the Founder of Academy for Church Planting and Leadership and the General Secretary and Director of Indian Institute of Inter Cultural Society; he is also a member of Evangelical Theological Society and Evangelical Missiological Society.

Yakubu Tanko Jakada is a faculty of the Baptist Seminary Kaduna Nigeria, he attended the International Peacemakers Program of Hartford Seminary, Hartford, Connecticut USA, and currently doing his PhD work in Intercultural Studies at Asbury Theological Seminary Wilmore, Kentucky in the United States.

Toshi Aier teaches History of Christianity at Clark Theological College, Aolijen, Mokokchung.